THE

CRY

AT

ZERO

Andrew Joron

COUNTERPATH PRESS / DENVER, COLORADO / 2007

THE

CRY

Selected Prose

AT

ZERO

Counterpath Press
Denver, Colorado
www.counterpathpress.org

Printed in the United States of America

Library of Congress Cataloging-in-Publication Data

Joron, Andrew.
The cry at zero : selected prose / Andrew Joron.
    p.   cm.
ISBN 978-1-933996-02-8 (pbk. : acid-free paper)
I. Title.
PS3560.O766C58   2007
818'.5409—dc22

                                    2006037258

CONTENTS

ACKNOWLEDGMENTS

Grateful acknowledgment is made to the editors of the magazines and anthologies in which these works first appeared: *apex of the M, Aufgabe, Bay Poetics, Central Park, English Language Notes, lingo, Natural History, Notus, Orpheus Grid, Parthenon West Review, P-Queue, 26,* and *Zyzzyva.*

"On Alexandrian Philosophy" was first published as the introduction to Will Alexander's book of essays *Towards the Primeval Lightning Field* (Oakland, California: O Books, 1998).

"On Neo-Surrealism" is an excerpt from the author's critical study *The Sun at Night: Transformations of Surrealism in American Poetry, 1966–1999* (New York: Black Square Editions, 2004).

The prose poems "Confession: On Method," "Fate Map," "First Drift," "The Inverted World," "Invol," "Masked Dialectic," "The Removes," and "The Revolution by Night" previously appeared in the author's collection *The Removes* (West Stockbridge, Massachusetts: Hard Press, 1999).

Special thanks to Garrett Caples who, while preparing Philip Lamantia's papers for archival evaluation, alerted me to the existence of Lamantia's abandoned poem-cycle *Tau*.

For her love and understanding, my deepest thanks go to Rose Vekony, la fleur de mon coeur.

THE

CRY

AT

ZERO

The Emergency

I

What good is poetry at a time like this? It feels right to ask this question, and at the same time to resist the range of predictable answers, such as: Poetry is useless, therein lies its freedom. Or, poetry has the power to expose ideology; gives a voice to that which has been denied a voice; serves as a call to action; consoles and counsels; keeps the spirit alive.

All of the above answers are true, yet somehow inadequate. This is because poetry cannot be anything other than inadequate, even to itself. Where language fails, poetry begins. Poetry forces language to fail, to fall out of itself, to become something other than itself—

A kind of topological fold or failure (called a "catastrophe" in mathematics) precedes the emergence—constitutes the emergency—of the New. If poetry "makes language new," then it must be defined as the *translation of emergency*. Even politically engaged poetry cannot escape this consequence. The abyssal language of poetry represents (translates) the *motion* of social change more than it does the *facts* of social change.

Language is a social construct, yet it was fashioned by no one in particular. Language continues to be haunted by this "no one." Indeed, the basic structures of language have more in common with molecular bonds than with human interactions.

To the extent that words are things, they cannot speak. (Speaking belongs to social action.) Poetry, before taking action, listens to the speechlessness of words.

Receiver of the sender who is "no one." (As the initial shading out of nothing, the sending of the longest amplitude—the deepest, the slowest—is always a lament.)

II

At this moment (late 2001), public space in the United States is bedecked with flags, colorfully curtaining the contradictions of the "war against terrorism," which is itself a higher, officially sanctioned form of terrorism.

"America stands united," yet remains a divided and antagonistic society, driven by capitalism's war of all against all. Such a society can achieve "unity" only through hatred of an external enemy. This is the utopian aspect of military campaigns.

But the euphoria of this newfound unity is fading fast. The screens have been repaired, but the picture still doesn't look right. Civil liberties have been curtailed, while new rights and benefits have been granted to the big corporations. Moreover, the "war of good against evil" seems to entail U.S. support for undemocratic regimes and clandestine organizations, hardly differing from those of the purported enemy, to the extent that such forces enable U.S. capital and influence to penetrate a given region of the world.

In the Mideast, in particular, acts of resistance to U.S. domination have grown increasingly desperate. Needless to say, no grievance could justify the atrocities committed on 9/11. These horrific acts constituted nothing less than crimes against humanity—to which the U.S. was obligated, morally and politically, not to respond in kind. A civilized nation would have investigated and prosecuted the crimes according to procedures laid down by international law. Instead, the U.S. chose to violate the law by conducting a war of annihilative vengeance, caring very little to discriminate between suspected terrorists and innocent bystanders.

—*only an inert and mechanical prose can accommodate these events*. It would be barbaric to write a poem about them, to use them for aesthetic purposes—

The United States, in its all-consuming pursuit of wealth and power, "has rained death and destruction on more people in more regions of the globe than any other nation in the period since the Second World War" (*Monthly Review*, November 2001). Violence of this order must take its toll on the life-world of the destroyer-nation itself. A harsh, acrid odor begins to seep through the walls, spoiling works of art and other fixtures of civilization.

In the case of America, this odor appears to be invigorating.—Adorno believed that any civilization guilty of mass murder must forfeit its right to cultural creation. As he famously declared, "To write poetry after Auschwitz is barbaric." In his view, aesthetic practices that once prefigured social emancipation now serve only to mask or to legitimate systemic violence. Here in America, however, "culture" has been reduced to a simple play of intensities, to the simultaneously brutal and sentimental pulsions of mass media. Any "legitimation function" would be superfluous: the American machine, with its proudly exposed components of Accumulation and Repression, has no need for such a carapace.

American poetry is a marginal genre whose existence is irrelevant to the course of Empire. Yet here, only here, at this very juncture between language and power, can the refused word come back to itself as the word of refusal, as the sign of that which cannot be assimilated to the system—

Word that opens a solar eye in the middle of the Night.

Opens, but fails to dispel the dark. Of necessity, perhaps, because it fails necessity itself. Opens, if only to make an O, an indwelling of zero, an Otherness.

The creative Word comes into its exile here, in the world's most destructive nation.

III

This poetic opening in the "real world" is a wonderful (meaning miraculous) wound, a sigh more than a sign. It has none of the decorative quality of the art of forgetting; this Word does not bring reconciliation. It affirms nothing but the negative truth of its non-identity. It does not communicate at all, except to announce the incommunicable, as abyssal groan, as *Ungrund*.

This shudder makes itself felt in the oldest, shamanic art, in labor turned against itself, toward the production of—the distribution of—[say here what spills spells: that Word that goes wanting]. Yet it also represents an expenditure that must be regulated. Polarized by the field of social struggle, poiesis is pulled at once toward the ornamental and the abyssal.

Ornament raises possibilities in order to restrict them. It has no hold, however, on the release of the Cry. The limited cannot attain the limitless, except by a *sudden break*.

Adorno himself conceded, some years after his initial statement, that "Perennial suffering has as much right to expression as a tortured man has to scream; hence it may have been wrong to say that after Auschwitz you could no longer write poems."

Yet the Cry involves more than a reflexive response to pain: it is an act of creation, a sign that the world is not equal to itself.

Haven't the very bones of language, in which meaning is always displaced from its object, the structure of a lament? Isn't this lament already evident in every self-separation, every self-exceeding motion of matter? What did Adorno know about the blues, and their ancient authority?

The blues, all blues, are the matrix of the world's subaltern cultures, an expression of triumph in defeat. The raising of the voiceless voice, *omnipresent roar of that river forced underground.*

(The more ancient the blues, the more collective the voice.)

Today's evidence: bare branches at the winter solstice, the turning point. The word to be awaited here.

Word beyond meaning—for that which triumphs in defeat is the Inexpressible, the joyous object of lament. All of language, as a mode of interaction that never is fully present to itself, amounts to the labor of producing this object.

The *emergence* of this object constitutes an *emergency* for any restricted economy of meaning. The privileged site of such an emergency in language is the poem, where something ontologically unprecedented springs forth: *Der Rätsel ist Reinentsprungenes* (the enigma is pure springing-forth), as Hölderlin testified.

This "enigma"—the poem's saying of the unsayable—arises from the interaction of a particular set of words, yet its enigmatic properties cannot be located among the properties of its constituent elements (i.e., the meanings of the words). The enigma springs forth purely at the level of interaction, and so exceeds the reality of the interacting elements themselves.

Indeed, scientists as well as poets now speculate that the origin of language itself was an "innovation" that "would have depended on the phenomenon of emergence, whereby a chance combination of preexisting elements results in something totally unexpected. The classic example of an emergent quality is water, most of whose remarkable characteristics are entirely unpredicted by those of its constituents, hydrogen and oxygen. Nonetheless, the combination of these ingredients gives rise to something entirely new, and expected only in hindsight." Thus, "we have to conclude that the appearance of language was not driven by natural selection" (*Scientific American*, December 2001)—instead, like water, language also is an emergent phenomenon, spontaneously springing forth as a pure enigma, an overflowing of reality, a surreality.

Recent studies of complex systems (from which the concept of emergence is derived) appear to confirm the surrealist insight into the poetic-revolutionary nature of reality. Investigations have shown that systems comprised of a large number of elements far from equilibrium are prone to beautiful convulsions called "phase transitions." In this process, chance associations within the system, after reaching a critical point, undergo spontaneous self-organization. At this point, the Novum—an unexpected, unprecedented superaddition to reality—emerges. Here is the dynamical equivalent of water flowing uphill: the system increases its complexity (and temporarily contravenes entropy) by incorporating chaos. *The origins of order are vertiginous*: by "riding" its own chaotic tendencies, the system propels itself to a higher level of organization. Complex systems, as one researcher[1] put it, are situated at the "edge of chaos."

Within the complex system of language, a word's meaning is "edged"—and chaotically conditioned—by the meanings of all other words. Communication attempts to crystallize this chaos by establishing fixed relations between the meanings of particular words. But such language-crystals melt and re-

---

1. Christopher Langton, an expert on self-reproducing automata, quoted in M. Mitchell Waldrop, *Complexity: The Emerging Science at the Edge of Order and Chaos* (Touchstone: New York, 1992).

form constantly in response to their (subjectively mediated) surroundings. (Complex systems are typically *open* systems to which rigid concepts of "inside" and "outside" do not apply. Such openness allows them to be extremely sensitive to changes in the environment.) In this process, communication proves susceptible to structural failure. The abyssal turbulence of language as a whole, always brimming beneath the surface of stabilized meaning, can initiate a spontaneous phase transition that accelerates words far beyond equilibrium, toward the condition of poetry.

Poetry is the self-organized criticality of the cry.

(The concept of "self-organized criticality" can be illustrated by pouring a quantity of sand onto a tabletop: the fallen particles will build up into a conical pile. This shape is the product of self-organization, for the pile maintains itself around a critical vertex, a balance-point between order and chaos. Once this critical point is reached, the effect of a single particle's impact on the pile no longer can be predicted. One particle may cause a chain reaction of cascades upon impact, while another may rest where it falls. Not only have the system's elements spontaneously organized themselves in reaction to an influx of energy, but the system as a whole has "tuned" itself toward a state of criticality, where single events have the widest possible range of effects.)

A poem tunes itself toward a state of criticality, a condition of language in which single words have the widest possible range of effects. No matter how the poem has been constructed, when poiesis has been achieved, the words of the poem leap spontaneously to a new interactive level (irreducible to any previous level), a level representing the self-organization of a cry emanating from nowhere and no one, but pervading all of language. What disequilibrium forces this *original cry* to wander through countless subsystems of meaning, always exceeding the capacities of each to contain it, until it finally surpasses the system of language itself?

IV

When laments are raised, they run together like water, collecting into a river that rushes toward an unknown ocean. They travel always in the direction of lengthening shadows, merging in the collectivity of night.

According to human-rights groups, the number of civilians (mostly women, children, and old people) killed by U.S. bombing in Afghanistan now equals the number of people killed by the terrorist attacks on 9/11. Once again, vengeful acts have taken the lives of three thousand innocent people. The U.S. has responded to a crime against humanity by inflicting another, equally atrocious one. Furthermore, the relentless bombing has halted the delivery of humanitarian aid, placing millions of refugees in imminent danger of disease and starvation.

Through the night of these sacred and profane wars of vengeance, the words of a poet must come together with those of others struggling for peace and social justice. Words of anger, argument, and analysis especially are needed, for these words lead to action. But the oldest, deepest oppositional words are those issued in lament. The lament, no less than anger, refuses to accept the fact of suffering. But while anger must possess the stimulus of a proximate cause—or else it eventually fades away—the lament has a universal cause, and rises undiminished through millennia of cultural mediation. Unlike anger, the lament survives translation into silence, into ruins.

Contemporary lyricism has been described as the "singing of song's impossibility." This, too, may be a version of the blues—whose strong ontological claim (to manifest the spontaneous emergence—or emergency—of an unprecedented Cry) now must be renewed.

Such a renewal would constitute an "ontological turn" away from the epistemological dilemmas of modern and postmodern poetics, where poetry is understood to emerge from the questioning of poetry. To the extent that a question anticipates its answer, it is unprepared to receive the Novum. That which is radically *other* does not reveal itself under interrogation.

The *deep blues*, then, are not a mode of questioning, but arrive in advance of doubt—and represent a negation more primary than doubt.

Here is the seed of all resistance. Here is its ratio:

O, the grieving vowel

———————————

zero, the mouth of astonishment

V

In a word, the uncanny reflection of an unfinished world.

Confession: On Method

I

I longed for the discovery of sound. My surroundings were evolving slowly toward recognition—no walls or people existed as yet, only their categories: the embryos of birds, the unopened eye of a window.

I had practiced the art of swooning—of allowing one's perceptions, previously exact and parallel as the folds of a curtain—

Swirl of coordinates, like the hem of a gown, to be gathered up, so as not to brush against—I was allowed to fall backward, into the arms of—But there is no word, no sound, to serve as object here.

My cry, withheld, was described by the arc that shone dimly—the limb of a letter, or starry Cross near the invention of writing.

Logos was a ghost, or mirror that held the whirlpool-image of its origin—so it was given to me, Word incarnate, compound of delirium, dissolving on my tongue—

A cistern, or sky, where sight was poured. Space was overloaded with aspects of vanishing: *Melancholia*, my visible mind, was shamed by its innocence in the face of obscurity.

Hooded, I had premeditated Time, a lesson in self-division.

There was divine mockery of my weakness, my fable about a spire of flesh; and the names that "blood sang."

What consonants answered the mystery of the vowels, in a chorus rising toward the bodiless? I lay disheveled, exposed beneath a dome.

Whatever I was, was written. Close to—closing to—a moment that was proximate, impervious, and final.

2

archaic torso : in shadow-rotation

equivalence, a burden : lost optic

a moving center : the Earth made weightless

the hidden : folds within simplicity

calculus, for what calling : between the veils

intervals, the Unanswering : exfoliant

of rending : of rendering

tears, through tears : gauze over gaze

terminus over term : Surrender

sunless, whose peaks : who speaks

solace : words given up to

no other, fused : refused

3

Telling the Silences, incendiary within every code.

—flight of the Alone to the Alone.

—attempted signature, leaking into structure: the hand memorious of the fires of its making.

Of logic, the unfastenings, joined at the vertex of all possible statements.

Of space & its responses, the endless recess. Realism that underlies the name, buried in its own transparency.

—coils everlasting through sensation's hollows, a shell of concentric hells.

Preliminary to blindness, revision. Form is given by that which it cannot contain.

—a blank page is the flag of a secret conflagration.

Turned inside out, so that flesh enspheres a central star.

Birthplace of the first displacement.

System of systems, where an Inhuman mechanism is learning to weep. Being absolutely porous, to absorb the mortal body.

Sites of abandonment stand for the letter A.

Asylum's analytic, accumulating zeroes, antinomies, atoms.

Unheard dissonance, whose harmonic arcs—curling across the Original void—fall sideways into lines of script.

—"after the end, before the beginning." Law that weighs its own likenesses, the ways of its release—

Language as Ghost Condensate

Does the way a poem is made have any relation to the way the world makes itself?

The answer, for the Romantics and especially for post-Romantics like the Surrealists, is emphatically *yes*! Both word and world participate in the miraculous production of something from nothing. Indeed, "something" (which Romantic philosophers deemed the Relative) emerges only as a kind of convulsion of "nothing" (otherwise known as the Absolute). Here, the impossible movement of the Absolute becomes a lightning-flash that "writes" both word and world.

This answer must be rejected, of course, by the dominant paradigm of innovative verse in the United States today, namely, the synthesis of Language poetry and the New York School. Within this paradigm, questions of poetic ontology are superseded by those of poetic epistemology: the substance of the word is considered as a social construct having no immediate relation to the substance of the world. Skepticism replaces enthusiasm; and poetic practice, once proclaimed to be a force of nature by the Romantics, is (re)socialized as a means to criticize *what is* rather than to create *what is not.*

However, these polarities are themselves historically conditioned and impermanent; another turn of the dialectic may bring them, if not into reconciliation, at least into agonistic embrace. (The very figure of such an embrace—the paradox—offers itself as a successor to metaphor and metonymy.)

Prior to the postmodern "linguistic turn," where the horizon of the sign receded to an unsurpassable distance, the equation between sign and *Sein*—or source of being beyond the sign—was recognized (by Hölderlin, Novalis, and other Romantics) as the foundation of poetic freedom. Art, no longer bound to its traditional social function of legitimating power, was free to abandon mimesis: what the poem presented was a primary reality beyond representation, expressing a truth as inexhaustible as the productions of nature itself.

As Hart Crane, one of the American inheritors of Romanticism, put it: "The writing of a poem is not—as the writing of a chemical equation is—intended to describe anything; instead, the poem *is the chemical reaction itself.*" As opposed to the aesthetics of the Classical period, which conceived the poem as a kind of machine operating according to strict rules of composition (Boileau), the Romantics and later modernists envisioned a nonmechanical, nonlinear form of motion common to the *poiesis* of both word and world, something like a turbulent fluid or a force-field.

Accordingly, the first Surrealist text, coauthored by Breton and Soupault, was entitled *The Magnetic Fields*; in this work, language circulates marvelously within an extrasocial pattern of energy. Likewise, Charles Olson (a poet whom the Language movement claims as one of its progenitors) asserted that "the poem is an energy-construct." And like the Surrealists, Olson believed that cosmic forces are given free play in the highest cultural constructs. As Olson wrote in his *Mayan Letters*, "a Sumer poem or Maya glyph is more pertinent to our purposes than anything else, because each of these peoples & their workers had forms which unfolded directly from content (said content itself a disposition toward reality which understood man as only force in field of force containing multiple other expressions)."

Olson, modeling his interpretation of the Mayan glyph on Pound/Fenollosa's creative misreading of the Chinese ideogram, was seeking a symbol for the "field of force" underlying both natural processes and the making of language. Similarly, Pound supported Fenollosa's conviction that the Chinese ideogram was a "vivid shorthand picture of the operations of nature." These operations were held to be complex and nonlinear; the ideogram clearly showed that the figuration of truth, whether scientific or poetic, "consists in following as closely as may be the actual and entangled lines of forces as they pulse through things."

Now, social constructivism, despite its elision of the cosmic, also understands language to be a complex, self-organizing system ("language knows more than we do"). Yet in constructivist theory and practice, the roots of this entangled system are traced to no deeper level than that of social interactions. Nonetheless, the picture of language as a system poised between order and chaos provides an opening for radical (extrasocial) ontology. Here, poetic "lines of force" point toward uninhabited wildernesses within language, toward removes of irreducible meaning—so that a poetic impulse will cause the system of language to exceed its own boundary conditions, and to undergo a phase transition toward the Unsayable.

Typically, any complex system undergoing a phase transition (whether a weather system transitioning to storm-life, or a language system transitioning to poetry) becomes turbulent (i.e., susceptible to unpredictable, nonlinear change) at all levels. In language, these mutating levels are equally semantic, syntactic, and sonic. Thus, a poetic "vortext" is generated semantically by paradox, syntactically by reflexivity, and sonically by echoic interference: *of air of air of air of error.*

Language is a self-exceeding system that can never be fully present to itself. It is a kind of "ghost condensate," existing everywhere and nowhere at once. As such, it demands a lyric practice capable of (once again) nerving the entangled ontologies of body and sky.

Fate Map

Pulling apart the lips of a white page reveals a curious network of fine bones, like those of an abstract bird, well documented in—

"The sung rotations of a shadowless mind," as the blind geometer referred to his theorems—

A body is composed of wounds, as a music of intervals, to defy its own proportions—retrieveless evidence that, in grieving—

Hollows, recesses. Dim cloaca. The wedded halves of darkness within a disarticulated word, *animalcule*—

Upon each of the seven portals, a social contract was imposed by violence, historically rising toward the eyes, the icy windows of the Law—

Nothing disturbs the clock's last hours, its membranes infiltrated with crimson inks, a growing stain on the horizon—

Interrogative sign: an unbreathed fragrance, closer than air—

Night comes from nothing, the oldest appellative. Withheld (still crowded with nerves)—

Folded at wrong angles. The linguistic plane whose coordinate points are elongated now to perfect cries—

Thus Earth's fixity is revised to a magnetic rose, a more dreamlike rate of fall—an atlas whose leaves have turned frail as human tissue—

Rest, remainder. The solace of an object will be its strange majority, its overwhelming sum—

The Inverted World

During the decline of the Roman Empire, it was believed that the Moon was the resting-place of forgotten dreams; and that the Moon's eastward motion caused an inaudible, deep melancholic tone to propagate through the aether.

—a late quietness, a null choir. Information continues to be exchanged between the spinning and the stationary worlds. Copyists continue to work in the burning libraries, producing Timeless pages, wraith-like fabulations . . .

"On the far side of the Moon, where the Earth is never visible, the inhabitants are embraced by living machines. Meeting in vast underground gardens, rhetoricians uphold the myth that human beings, indeed all life, originated on the Moon, and that *the Moon itself must be the True Earth.*

It is argued that the True Earth, now airless and sterile, was stripped of its biosphere in some primeval conflict . . . "

The old world's thinnest crescent, a whisper of light. Photograph of an inverted birth, widely distributed, showing the figure of a man ascending a ladder, feetfirst, toward the rocky floor of Heaven.

Winter was followed by autumn—another error in transcription. The wind was disassembled [dissembled?] into [through?] so many voices . . .

Nothing equals anything: an elegant proof of zero's secret marriage to infinity. Pallid union of Indivisibles, kept safe inside the curve of a knife.

A feather falling in a vacuum.

N. Armstrong's words, spoken centuries ago, as he stepped—the First Man—onto the ground of the True Earth:

"We Americans have outlived the end of the world. The great cataclysms of history all appear to have ended; our fragmented identities are carried forward in time only by attenuating waves of radio noise. As the Indian shamans predicted, the land called Turtle Island has been repopulated by ghost-tribes, simulacra of the living. Nevertheless, a few among us have sensed, with the shadow-sensations available to ghosts, a desire to return to our true home in the Moon."

Terror Conduction

1. Duncan's "Orders"

Poetry is not innocent when it comes to war.

The "autonomy" of art under capitalism finds its limit-condition, and its inverted image, in oppressive social class divisions enforced by state violence. The effect of this violence seeps into, stains even as it sustains, the very form of free invention.

Not only is high culture supported by barbaric activities, but the poetic act—according to Nietzsche, Bataille, and certain postmodernists—itself makes a war of and on creation.

Such was the signal, or cry, emitted by philosophy at the moment of its separation from myth: "War is the father of all things." This saying of Heraclitus, which posits the identity of *logos* and violence, was revised by Empedocles, who in his poem *On Nature* contended that "All things are composed equally of love and strife." Nevertheless, an agonism at the heart of existence is here laid bare, a warlike interaction best revealed and preserved in poetic language.

Among contemporary American poets, none has explored the idea that poetry is implicated in war more deeply than Robert Duncan. A magisterial study by Nathaniel Mackey, *Gassire's Lute*,[1] demonstrates that, in Duncan's practice, "Poetry is both haunted and sustained by, 'hounded' and sustained by, recollections and confirmations of this primal taint [of violence]." For Duncan, "The poem is a war and the war is a poem" (GL 6:157).

In reference to H. D.'s wartime *Trilogy*, Duncan wrote that "It is the 'unalterable purpose' of the poem to convert the War to its own uses . . . the War is not to be taken for granted as simply an economic or political opportunity or as a disorder, but it is also a Mystery play or dream projection to be witnessed and interpreted, to be endured in order to be understood. The War rises from the dramatic necessity" (cited in GL 6:152–53). Ultimately, both poetry and war are understood through Duncan's gnostic Freudianism to be expressions of a timeless struggle between Eros and Thanatos, a war that generates the historical unfolding of the World-Poem itself.

As Mackey shows, Duncan's humanistic outrage—both at the suffering entailed by war and at the warmakers' base motivations of profit and power—is complicated by a belief in the necessity of conflict in history and poetry alike. Mack-

---

1. *Gassire's Lute* was published serially in the literary magazine *Talisman*, nos. 5–7 (1990–1991). Citations here refer to issues and pages of this magazine.

ey points out that "War is also an internal characteristic of [Duncan's poetry], a fact of life at work within each word of which the poem is made" (GL 6:156). In *Bending the Bow*, Duncan invokes the hermetic invention of the bow and the lyre as a simultaneous event, a "*a connexion working in both directions.*"[2] Thus, the lyric instrument is confounded with an instrument of war.

This "*connexion*" also is evident in the African legend of Gassire's lute, which Duncan cites at a crucial moment in his poem "Orders" (BB 77–80). The legend tells of a fierce warrior named Gassire who is impatient to inherit his father's kingship. Gassire consults a wise man about how to hurry his inheritance. The wise man instructs Gassire to enter battle with a lute slung on his back. During the battle, Gassire's sons, fighting at his side, are slain and the lute is stained with their blood. After the battle, Gassire is exiled from his native city of Wagadu, whose citizens have grown weary of war. Gassire takes the bloodstained lute with him into the desert and one night is awakened to hear it singing of its own volition. That very night, Gassire's father dies and the city of Wagadu vanishes from the face of the earth. The legend does not lend itself to easy interpretation, although it is clear that the lyric gift comes at the price of blood.

Duncan significantly revises the legend in his poem "Orders," a response to the U.S. invasion of the Dominican Republic. Here, Duncan describes the Marines as "hired and conscripted killers" acting "against the power of an idea, against / / Gassire's lute,   the song / / of Wagadu, household of the folk, / / commune of communes / / hidden seed in the

2. *Bending the Bow* (New York: New Directions, 1968), p. iv. Henceforth cited as BB.

hearts of men // and in each woman's womb   hidden" (BB 77). The song of Gassire's lute now is held to represent a hidden, but still extant, community—one, moreover, whose status has been heightened to that of an archetypal "commune of communes." It is the "power" of this "idea," articulated by the song of Gassire's lute, that constitutes the real target of the U.S. invasion.

Mackey explains this blatant revision of the legend as a "symptom" of Duncan's declared intention in the poem to "put aside // whatever I once served of the poet, master / of enchanting words and magics. . . . For the Good . . . the good of the people, // the soul's good" (BB 77), so that Gassire's lute, that magical destroyer of community, finally is made to sing for the "household of the folk." Duncan, in Mackey's view, is attempting here to recast his poetic character from elitist magician to populist servant of the Good (though as Mackey observes, the attempt ends in the assumption of an even more "oracular, rhapsodic voice" [GL 5:93]).

At the high point of the poem, Duncan defines the Good as merely one aspect of an interrelated cosmos: "There is no // good a man has in his own things except // it be in the community of every thing; // no nature he has // but in his nature hidden in the heart of the living, // in the great household" (BB 79). This claim—that the nature of each particular thing is determined by its relation to the whole—is a commonplace of occult lore as well as of dialectical philosophy. With his next breath, however, Duncan makes the statement that is crucial to integrating the meaning of this poem entitled "Orders": "The cosmos will not // dissolve its orders at man's evil." That is, the attributes (whether good or evil) of individual beings are secondary to their true, albeit "hidden," nature, which springs from the interrelatedness of all beings. The indissoluble orders of the cosmos consist of these secret linkages: the presence of All within Each is the primary fact of nature.

Moreover, none of the actions of individual beings, including their coming into being and passing away, can alter the pattern of the Whole: in the poem, Duncan quotes Proclus to emphasize this point: "'That which is corrupted is corrupted with reference to / itself but not destroyed with reference to the universe.'" (BB 79, from Proclus's commentary on Plato's *Timaeus*). Change occurs only with reference to the particular, not to the universal. The corollary of this insight is that neither "man's evil" nor man's good can change the world.

Wagadu, therefore, can be described as a "commune of communes," as the very paradigm of interrelatedness, because it represents the cohabitation of good and evil in our hearts. If Duncan, contrary to the original legend of Gassire's lute, identifies the song of the lute with "the song//of Wagadu," it is because he maintains a gnostic belief in the embrace of Eros and Thanatos—which brings him to affirm the secret relation between "man's evil" and aesthetic beauty. He makes the following equation: " . . . rage, / grief, dismay transported—but these / are themselves transports of beauty! The blood//streams from the bodies of his sons / to feed the voice of Gassire's lute" (BB 79).

The blood that is spilled by "man's evil" cannot dissolve the orders of the cosmos, but instead flows into the "voice of Gassire's lute," that is, into the changeless beauty of that pattern of patterns, that interrelation of love and strife "hidden in the heart of the living."

2. Bataille's Disorders

Ineluctably, Duncan's open form closes upon itself. Here, the commotion of the parts is stilled at the height of the Whole, whose pattern persists eternally. Creation is indestructible, inasmuch as creation and destruction become mirror-aspects of one another.

Yet the formlessness of a bloodstain seeps out of this well-rounded order. The stain possesses no pattern, and resembles nothing other than itself.

This stain stands for the Chaos that cannot be reconciled to Order. In a cosmos ruled by the self-resemblance of hidden orders, what place does non-resemblance have? As a return of the repressed, it seeps scandalously from that line of darkness that divides the self-mirroring symmetries. Its asymmetrical trace provokes the suspicion that, as Adorno put it, "the Whole is the untrue."

Or, in Bataille's words (from *Documents*), "affirming that the universe resembles nothing and is only *formless* amounts to saying that the universe is something like a spider or spit," something, that is, "that has no rights in any sense and gets itself squashed everywhere, like a spider or an earthworm." For Bataille, the cosmos *will* dissolve its orders at man's evil.

Yet Bataille's fetishization of evil itself represents only the mirror-reversal of an officially sanctioned moral ideology. Bataille, like Duncan, strives poetically to inscribe destruction within creation but, like Duncan, falls prey to anthropomorphism by projecting the antagonisms of the human heart onto the workings of the cosmos.

Moreover, the binary logic of mutually conditioning and implicating powers ("good vs. evil") can only produce what Bataille himself has called a "restricted economy." Evil remains imprisoned by its negation of the Good. Only a sovereign economy, one that is free to exceed its own limit-conditions, can do justice to the fact of non-resemblance.

3. A Cosmo-Political Treatise

The concept of a system that does not resemble itself, that supports itself by expenditure, that ultimately *cannot contain itself* has been formulated not only in the philosophy of Bataille, but in physics, with Nobel Prize–winner Ilya Prigogine's theory of "dissipative structures." Prigogine's theory recognizes that complex systems (both living and nonliving) are *structured by dissipation*: the organization of such systems arises from their openness to disorganization.[3]

Dissipative structures appear to be poised, more or less precariously, between chaos and order. Indeed, they maintain or increase their orderliness by incorporating disorder: here, random fluctuations incite (r)evolutionary development. Structuration results not from a "top-down" determinism directed by the Whole, but from a "bottom-up" indeterminism inherent to the agitation of the parts.

The agitation of the parts has revolutionized the Whole at least five times in cosmic history: namely, in the nonlinear series leading from atomic, to molecular, to biological, to social, to linguistic systems of interaction. Through these suc-

3. Ilya Prigogine and Isabelle Stengers, *Order Out of Chaos* (New York: Bantam Books, 1984).

cessive levels, new and unprecedented properties of matter have emerged—properties that cannot be reduced to those of the interacting elements themselves. For example, the atoms that compose water are not themselves fluid; the components of life are not themselves alive; the elements of language in isolation are meaningless: in each case, a form of interactivity poised between order and chaos[4] has resulted in an ontological breakthrough. In this new version of materialism, the mirror-relation between macrocosm and microcosm is shattered, and the radical *non-resemblance* between the faces, the phases, of existence is demonstrated.

Equilibrium = stasis (or death). Therefore, systems of emergence must maintain themselves in a state of disequilibrium, or emergency. To accomplish this, such systems must remain *open* to their environments: by doing so, they will internalize chaos, circulating the non-identical as identity. The circulatory apparatus must be composed of positive (change-promoting) and negative (change-inhibiting) feedback loops, complexly entangled. Furthermore, the complexity of such systems cannot be reduced to any one element of the system. No part can determine or represent the Whole. And conversely, the *emergency of being* can be maintained only if the structure of the Whole does not control the interaction of the parts.

This cosmo-political law holds for human societies as well: basic forms of organization (including language) that emerge from social interaction cannot be reduced to the intentionality of group or individual actors; at the same time, these self-organizing (agency-transcending) forms remain susceptible

4. "A single drop of water is a seething melee of order and disorder, with structures constantly forming and breaking up within it." *New Scientist* no. 2546 (April 2006), p. 32.

to disequilibria (emergencies) set in motion by human agency. Here, it is relevant to cite the thoroughgoing attempt to "incorporate Prigogine's insights into the study of human history" undertaken by Manuel De Landa in his book *A Thousand Years of Nonlinear History*.[5] De Landa's aim is "not simply to assume that society forms a system, but to account for this systematicity as an emergent property of some dynamical process."[6]

As De Landa writes, "Even though the world is inherently nonlinear and far from equilibrium, its [socioeconomic] homogenization meant that those areas that had been made uniform began *behaving objectively* as linear equilibrium structures, with predictable and controllable properties. In other words, Western societies transformed the objective world (or some areas of it) into the type of structure that would 'correspond' to their theories."[7] Inevitably, attempts to freeze the structure of the world through the imposition of globalized systems of power are defeated by reality's "inherent" nonlinearity. The rights of what De Landa calls "self-organized heterogeneity" are reasserted as the interaction of the parts bursts the integument of the Whole; abruptly, the world-system undergoes a "phase transition," moving from a frozen to a fluid state.

4. The Poetics of Emergency

At the present moment, we are witnessing a historic phase transition from a frozen world-system, characterized by the Cold War's equilibristic balance of power, to a more fluid sys-

5. Manuel De Landa, *A Thousand Years of Nonlinear History* (New York: Zone Books, 1997), p. 278.

6. Ibid., p. 270.

7. Ibid., p. 273.

tem characterized by geopolitical multipolarity. All efforts by a vestigial superpower to impose a Law of Resemblance upon this newly emerging system have so far met with failure.

In a system of sufficient complexity, causality is always local, never global: the fluid (or nonlinear) interactions that are a defining feature of complexity come to resist the freezing effect of global directives. *At the present moment, Empire is opposed by Swarm.* Resistance to U.S. imperialism now is manifested by a leaderless swarm of actors and organizations. The Swarm often takes the form of self-organized networks linked by nodes, no one of which can "see" or control the organization in its entirety. Most conspicuously, terrorist networks take this form; however, swarming is increasingly exhibited by other political movements (such as the Zapatistas in Mexico) as well.

Researchers at the Rand Corporation, a government-sponsored think tank, have studied the features of such networks in the hope of finding ways to counteract them: "The rise of networks means that power is migrating to nonstate actors, because they are able to organize into sprawling multiorganizational networks (especially 'all-channel' networks, in which every node is connected to every other node) more readily than can traditional, hierarchical, state actors. . . . Information-age threats are likely to be more diffuse, dispersed, multidimensional, nonlinear, and ambiguous than industrial-age threats."[8]

The researchers identify the "swarming" capability of such networks as the most serious threat of all. Swarming, they

8. John Arquilla and David Ronfeldt, *Networks and Netwars* (Santa Monica: Rand Corporation, 2001), pp. 1–2.

THE CRY AT ZERO

write, "is quite different from traditional mass- and maneuver-oriented approaches to conflict. . . . [It] is designed mainly around the deployment of myriad, small, dispersed, networked maneuver units. Swarming occurs when the dispersed units of a network of small (and perhaps some large) forces converge on a target from multiple directions. The overall aim is *sustainable pulsing*—swarm networks must be able to coalesce rapidly and stealthily on a target, then dissever and disperse, immediately ready to recombine for a new pulse. . . . The Chechen resistance to the Russian army and the Direct Action Network's operations in the anti–World Trade Organization 'Battle of Seattle' both provide excellent examples of swarming behavior."[9]

Swarming, in other words, maximizes the advantage of *formlessness* over form, undermining and even toppling what De Landa calls "linear equilibrium structures" through nonlinear action. Because such action is self-organizing and self-producing (or, in the terminology of complexity theory, *autopoietic*), it is liable to occur spontaneously at all levels of social organization. Not only does Swarm threaten Empire's monuments and armies, but its linguistic "linear equilibrium structures" as well. At the level of language, swarming is a sign of poetic activity.

While the dominant ideology attempts to globalize control of language, and thus to equilibrate meaning, language itself remains a complex system poised between order and chaos, susceptible to poetic convulsion. In poetic language, linear equilibrium structures of meaning become the targets of swarming attacks. Lines of poetic force converge upon a unit of meaning from multiple directions, in an ever-renew-

9. Ibid., p. 12.

ing play of pulses that dissever and recombine the relations of sense and sensation. In this way, the poetic act breaks the (ideologically imposed) mirror-symmetry between word and world.[10]

Here, Duncan's "connexion" between the bow and the lyre—the instrument of war and the instrument of song—becomes legible once again. However, the Heraclitean X of the equation must be revised: it is not war, but disequilibrium that is the progenitor of all. The poetic word is the latest extension of that series of broken symmetries that made the world.

In poetry, then, meaning exceeds its limits and becomes, at best, a mode of "terror conduction."[11] (The apparition of the sublime, as Kant and the Romantics defined it, brings about the structural failure of meaning: in his "Analytic of the Sublime," Kant emphasized its "chaos, . . . its wildest and most irregular disorder," which induces an "*astonishment* amounting almost to terror."[12] From Romanticism to postmodernism, the poetic act has always conducted language toward this opening.)

Yet where the bow *inflicts*, the lyre *inflects*: creation re-creates destruction as an Opening to Otherness. This abyssal passage will be negotiated by a subject without identity (that

10. Even formalist procedures in poetry must engage in symmetry-breaking to avoid mechanical motion: to retain poetic value, any procedure that stabilizes meaning in one direction must destabilize it in another.

11. The phrase "terror conduction" is taken from the title of a poem by Philip Lamantia, who originally included it in his poem-cycle *Tau* (an unpublished or "destroyed work" from 1955). For further discussion of *Tau*, see the final essay in this volume.

12. Immanuel Kant, *The Critique of Judgement*, trans. J. C. Meredith (Oxford: Clarendon Press, 1952), pp. 92 and 120.

is, one standing ecstatically outside the "linear equilibrium structure" of I = I).

Gassire's lute, as soon as it is stained with the blood of war, begins singing *of its own accord*, playing without need of a player. The lyric instrument refuses to serve as the instrument of agency: unlike the bow, the lyre undergoes metamorphosis once it has been stained by, inscribed by, suffering. This metamorphosis marks the advent of poetic autonomy.

The image of *a bloodstained lute that plays itself* recasts, in mythic terms, the concept of the self-organized criticality of the cry. Here, "the system [of singing, of signing] tunes itself towards optimum sensitivity to external inputs . . . towards the critical point where single events have the widest possible range of effects."[13] Whatever enters language at this pitch must circulate chaotically as a form of emergency.

The precondition of truth, according to Adorno, is that which gives a voice to suffering. However, the imperative of lyric—as the *ekstasis* of lament—is not to preserve suffering in a reified crystal, but instead to *move with suffering*, to trace its cry against its own condition as a movement toward something other than itself: Utopia, or Wagadu.

13. Paul Cilliers, *Complexity and Postmodernism* (New York: Routledge, 1998), p. 97.

Divinations of the Vortex(t)

"Because free will participates in pure accident, self-knowledge comes to resemble ornithomancy [divination based on the flight of birds]."

—IGNAZ MEES

"The sphere of *fa'l* or omens was enriched by the transition of the Arabs from a nomadic to a sedentary culture, while preserving nevertheless its original structure, especially where ornithomancy was concerned."

—*Encyclopedia of Islam*

1 February 2003. Divination of the errant flight of the *colombe*, or dove.

Why shouldn't the people of the Middle East, living under the oppression of the United States and its partner Israel, receive the news of the *Columbia* space shuttle disaster as a sign from the heavens? The shuttle, an important symbol of U.S. military and technological prowess, vanished in a puff of smoke with the first Israeli astronaut on board. Terrorist groups must have dreamed of destroying this symbolic target, flying far beyond the reach of any weapons available to them. Their only recourse was to wield the weapon of faith, to pray for the shuttle's destruction—and now it seems that such prayers were answered. The craft broke apart over the state of Texas, homeland of President Bush; in fact, one of the earliest sightings of the smoke trail was reported from the town of Palestine, Texas. This chain of chance could have been fashioned only by the hand of divinity: Allah, too, is a terrorist.

Whether by accident or divine intervention, a national monument has fallen—this time on the eve of a U.S.-driven imperialist war aimed at appropriating the world's second largest storehouse of oil. The U.S., as the world's only superpower, feels free to claim these resources; and what force can restrain it from doing so? Perhaps only the hand of Allah, which now has manifested itself through this symbolic action (no matter that innocent lives were lost, that the astronauts themselves were engaged in a nonmilitary, scientific mission). What omen more potent than this, at a moment when the nation is poised for war, could be scattered across the skies of America? Even if the event is ascribed to nothing more than natural causes, one Message hangs in the air: the technological power—and, by implication, the war machine—of the U.S. is not invincible.

The ominous sky-sign over Texas delivers a further blow to the nation's confidence and its resolve to make war (at least to the extent that elite, as well as popular, opinion relies on the interpretation of signs and portents). At the same time, the strongest portent against war surely is presented by the people in their millions, demonstrating in every major city of the world. If not for these massive, historically unprecedented protests, the U.S. invasion of Iraq likely would have been launched much sooner.

Yet the demonstrations are an earthly phenomenon, lacking the uncanny quality of a celestial sign. The shuttle's crew was returning, after all, from "the other side of the sky." Under their eyes, all horizons had met. Despite the nationalist pride associated with space programs, there's something subversive about viewing the Earth from space, where no national boundaries are visible. During his stay at the International Space Station, the Israeli astronaut was moved to speak of how "fragile" the Earth looked. That sentiment has been echoed by many previous space travelers. And somehow it always conjures the image of an ecologically harmonious, economically equitable society—the only one appropriate to such an encompassing vantage point. What terrorism, what brutal occupation of the soul, prevents us from bringing home this news?

•

Systems fail. Often the failure results from a peculiar constellation of precipitating factors, a sequence of events aligned by chance or *hasard* (words anciently understood to be synonymous with "Fate"). In such cases, randomness momentarily acquires a structure, an arrow-shape that pierces the meshwork of a system's sustaining feedback loops. Convulsively, then, an avalanche or a heart attack occurs.

This *structure of randomness* corresponds to what the Surrealists called "objective chance." As a force of nature that only now is beginning to be recognized and researched (especially in the new sciences of chaos and complexity), *l'hasard objectif* exerts creative as well as destructive power: indeed, the birth of the Universe itself is thought to have resulted from a random "vacuum fluctuation."

Randomness is the serial aspect of the Unconditioned, which may be defined as a state of negativity so absolute that it cannot keep from negating even itself. This kind of *absolute feedback*, however, brings about a fatal complication: Nothing must issue forth as Something. For non-being is not a self-same uniformity, but has its own contingent contours, its own localities and drifts, flowing in advance of time and space toward self-division.

A world composed of accidents, whose very essence is accident, cannot be equal to itself, but must exceed itself at every turn. What began as the spontaneous outspilling of a zero-point (or singularity) has carried its turbulence onward to errancies as unlikely as the writing of this sentence, the very shapes of whose letters delineate a graph of structured randomness. (That is to say: language is not predicated on the existence of meaning, but is an unpredictable outcome of a world that produced first fire, then birds.)

Structured randomness can emerge only in a universe that has lost its equilibrium, whose contents, cascading into an abyss, *swerve*—much as the ancient atomists imagined—and stray into one another's path, thus engaging in strange, and strangely intricate, relations. Atoms, of course, are no longer viewed as simple entities but as complex systems in their own right. Upon closer inspection, they blur into fields of force, consisting finally of modulations *of the vacuum itself.* The fundamental forces, then, are irritations of emptiness, pieces of a symmetry broken when the singularity (an impossible object poised exactly at the meeting-point of zero and infinity) spontaneously exploded.

As the cosmologist Martin Rees has pointed out, "There is an analogy here with a 'phase transition,' such as the familiar phenomenon of water turning into ice. When the inflationary era ended, space itself (the 'vacuum') underwent a drastic change. The fundamental forces—gravitational, nuclear, and electromagnetic—all 'froze out' as the temperature dropped, fixing their values in a manner that can be considered 'accidental,' just like the pattern of ice crystals when water freezes."[1]

If these events could be reversed, then started again from the zero-point, an entirely different set of fundamental forces would "freeze out." Rees and other cosmologists speculate that vacuum fluctuations may generate an infinity of randomly configured universes, most of them failing to organize beyond an initial "phase transition" and melting quickly back into nothingness. The fundamental forces in our own Universe, too, have intensities produced purely by accident. In our case, these arbitrary values have lined up like winning lottery numbers, yielding stars, planets, life, and mind: a fact that some philosophers interpret as evidence of divine "fine tuning," but that Surrealists, as visionary nihilists, can and should cite as an effect of OBJECTIVE CHANCE.

•

Amazing aleatory alignments can revolutionize, not only the mind (as narrated in Breton's *Nadja* and *L'amour fou*), but the material organization of the Universe itself.

1. Rees, *Just Six Numbers: The Deep Forces that Shape the Universe* (New York: Basic Books, 2000), p. 169.

The "delirium" of matter is manifested when random fluctuations provoke an interactive system to freeze or melt or boil over. In the ensuing phase transition, elements of the system spontaneously reorganize around the infiltration of chaos and, against all odds, derive a pattern from it. At this cusp of convulsive beauty, unpredictable—and ultimately *fantastical*—new properties are seen to emerge. Moreover, such emergences (emergencies) occur only at the level of interaction, and cannot be attributed to the interacting elements themselves (one obvious example is the emergence of life from nonliving elements). This chance-inspired reorganization of matter constitutes a *Novum*, as the utopian philosopher Ernst Bloch called it: a superaddition to reality, a surreality.

The more sensitive, the more susceptible a system is to the reshaping influence of chance, the greater its complexity. Storm-swirls, termites' nests, human moods and musings: such hierarchies of structured randomness are found at every level of objective, as well as subjective, reality. Systems of this kind are poised on the edge of chaos, and draw upon the surrounding turbulence as a source of developmental possibilities. As one group of researchers recently put it, "environmental randomness can act as the '*imagination of the system*,' the raw material from which structures arise. Fluctuations can act as seeds from which patterns and structures are nucleated and grow."[2]

Thus, the new science of complexity confirms and extends Breton's doctrine of *l'hasard objectif*. In conjunction with the practice of "pure psychic automatism," non-human nature also creates and complicates itself by free association. The ir-

2. S. Camazine et al., *Self-Organization in Biological Systems* (Princeton: Princeton University Press, 2001), p. 26 (my emphasis).

repressible upsurges, and insurgencies, of the unconscious mind have their correlate in the objective world's welter of marvelously ordered accidents.

Now, actions compelled by logic or linear causality cannot be regarded as "free," for they are merely the inevitable consequences of their initial conditions. In comparison, the relation between cause and effect in complex systems is *non-linear* (local causes bring about unpredictable global effects). As a result, the impetus of the Prime Mover must relinquish all system-directing power, as swarms of locally interacting elements produce holistic structures randomly and spontaneously, without coordination at the level of the system as a whole. The law-giving *Logos* cannot be preserved; Agency dissipates like a cloud.

Only that action without aim or antecedent is free.

•

By chance, two books of dissimilar content have been placed together on the same shelf: *Free Will*, authored by Craig Watson (Roof, 2000), and *Free Will*, edited by Gary Watson (Oxford, 1982). (In both cases, the first letter of the originator's forename strives—in vain—to complete a circle, perhaps representing the failure of writing to achieve a closed system.)

The printing on the spine of the later book reads as follows:

free will / craig watson / ROOF

The printing on the spine of the earlier book reads as follows:

Watson / Free Will / *Oxford*

Free Will is, on one hand, the title of a collection of four long poems, or poem-sequences, by a man named Watson. *Free Will* is, on the other hand, the title of a collection of eleven philosophical essays introduced and edited by a man named Watson.

Who is Watson? He is a man responsible for a book entitled *Free Will.*

Watson is a man who fears that "we may seem like puppets or machines; in a different simile, our behavior is like the 'falling rain'" (*Free Will*, page 1).

Watson also observes that "our collective fingerprints glow like a searchlight" (*Free Will*, page 11).

When rain falls on the calm surface of a pond, rings of wavelets radiate from the site of each drop's impact. As they expand, the rings (depending on the frequency of impact and the area of the pond) intersect one another. The resulting interference patterns are evidence—the collective fingerprints—of a process that is both random and structured. Human puppets or machines, though lacking free will, might possess such thought patterns.

But if we lack free will, Watson argues, our behavior is "not ours, not self-directed . . . we have no 'insides': we are in the relevant sense 'empty'" (*FW* 14). "Or is there a greater emptiness beyond emptiness," Watson wonders, pointing out that "every identity [is] bisected by material and method / whatever one is to itself" (*FW* 51).

Identity, whose inherent emptiness is reflected in the tautological proposition 1 = 1, requires a "greater emptiness beyond emptiness" in order to distinguish itself from zero. Therefore, whatever is identical to itself is already "bisected by [the] material and method" of oneness.

"Whatever one is to itself" cannot be known, because as soon as one reflects itself, it must turn into something other than itself. The equal sign, far from being an assertion of identity, necessarily divides one into two. At the same time, Watson implies that free will, inasmuch as it requires "self-directed" behavior, cannot exist unless the proposition "I = I" is true. Free will marks the difference between the I and not-I: it enables the self to exist as a closed system, as the cause of its own activity.

But where, among the series of causes that compose the natural world, can this autonomous ego insert itself without sacrificing its status as a self-possessing, "self-directed" agent—that is, without becoming just another link in the chain? "The problem of free will," Watson admits, "is part of the problem of finding room in the world for ourselves" (14). Later, Watson also remarks, "but some architecture was designed to be uninhabited" (68).

The design for the house of the autonomous ego, in particular, stipulates that its foundation be suspended in midair. "Free will" is truly free only to the extent that it proceeds from an initial, uncaused point within a causal series. This position, however, always has been reserved for an omnipotent deity, an "unmoved Mover." As Watson testifies, "The truth, of course, is that God (traditionally conceived) is the only free agent without qualification. . . . Human beings are only more or less free agents, typically less" (110). Apparently we are "more or less" marionettes of some kind, finally incapable, in Watson's phrase, of "that convulsion known as free will" (51). The self can experience absolute freedom only by way of mystical dissolution: "In ecstasy," Watson writes, "one pictures god about to squeeze the globe in an ancient but careless hand" (62).

6 March 2003. Divination of the vertiginous vortex(t).— Reading is perhaps the most subtle kind of writing.

•

Freedom is opposed to causality only in a closed system. All possible states of such a system are stabilized around a central attractor (for example, the oscillations of a pendulum). Free or spontaneous perturbations tend to be inhibited by the "pull" of the attractor (which is not a physical entity but an imaginative construct used for visualizing the behavior of a system, i.e., the shape of its causality). Here causality often takes the form of a circle or spiral. By contrast, in a system that opens itself to its environment, thereby incorporating random fluctuations, the shape of causality becomes nonlinear or "strange."

A strange attractor represents the merging of freedom and causality through structured randomness, where the ordering of elements is highly complex yet, at the same time, *unexpected and uncompelled.* Strangely attracted elements function not as impediments to one another's freedom (as, for example, individuals living under the privatizations and privations of capitalism) but as the facilitators of a mutually empowering struggle against closure, equilibrium, and death.

20 March 2003. To surrender to the violence of empire is to "choose what has been chosen" (*Free Will*, page 41). Today I, along with 1,400 other citizens, have been jailed in San Francisco for protesting the U.S. attack on Iraq. The arresting officer scrawled on my citation the words "REFUSAL TO OBEY."

•

6 September 2001. On the eve of her eighty-first birthday, Barbara Guest told me that "poets are chained to the impossible." This morning I brought her sunflowers and she quoted her lecture about growing up "under the shadow of Surrealism." This helped me to understand her earlier statement: Poets, it seems, are committed to a shadow that lengthens paradoxically *towards* the sun. Guest joins the Surrealists in seeking "the gold of time."

•

The transcendent Impossible can never come into being; the transformative Impossible, however, is the very action of coming into being. As Zeno demonstrated, time emerges from the impossible unity of being and not-being. To paraphrase Guest: poets are bound to that aspect of reality that cannot be reconciled with itself.

•

What is not is not the same as itself. The sunflower bends its head compassionately over the violation of that shadow.

Invol

Just as Chaos keeps its hidden orders—assuming that Beauty is beyond scale—if, & only if, its iteration is driven to Fury— So you have crosst my Tongue with the oldest knife.

Skepticism must ban the sight of Utopia: a straight line is the deepest labyrinth. Natural language has no author. The reddening of the landscape coincides with the movements of a clock.

Fascicle 1

The first line was completely crossed out, the second barely legible. The words were enumerative and blood-linked. Each possessed a shadow that hovered over us in the shape of a hand; abode of a star-gripped paralysis repeated in the gestures of Inhuman objects.

Fascicle 2

The terms were perfect sections of the voice, skewed in consequence of a dreamt assassination. The letters, neither flame-like, nor flower-like in that world without sound, were aligned within a lacerating machinery. Denuded, then left to wander through rooms of interlocking narrative.

Do immeasurable spaces exist inside one point? Here, you have painted the walls to purify my eyes, littered the floor with objects too cold to touch. Yet I am consoled by your philosophy of the Infinite Cage.

The Missing Body

[lettre par avion à Charles Borkhuis]

Dear Charles:

In your letter, sent from the Rue du Dragon in Paris, you sought to rescue the poetic image by teaching it to swim dialectically.

I still think that an image swims best when it is close to drowning. This feeling of struggle, of something vital being *at stake* in the poem, is implicit in the neo-Romanticism of your definition of the renewed or "critical" image.

You wrote that "the critical image makes reference to its processes and inner workings as it proceeds, and refuses development without transformation. To this extent, the critical image is an interrupted image that is self-referential and self-transformative."

What transformation ever proceeded without a desperate and

convulsive thrashing of limbs? It is not poetic *jouissance* that is interrupted, but only a conventionalized linearity.

Like you, I am inspired by the possibilities of an encounter between late Surrealism and Language poetry. One meets the other at the exact place that each believes is impossible to occupy. For Surrealism, the only thing that was unthinkable was that imagination should have a limit. For Language poetry, many more things are unthinkable, but chief among them is the idea that language is something other than a social construct.

I have always felt that Surrealism's absolutism, its will-to-totality (exemplified by Breton's "supreme point" where oppositions, including life and death, are reconciled) was an ideological holdover: how can you truly assassinate God if you continue to venerate his skeleton in the form of the principle of the identity of opposites?

Here is where Language poetry's insistence on the principle of non-identity and non-reconciliation (with reference to Adorno's "the whole is the untrue") proves indispensable. Yet the defeat of ideological strategies of unity and closure (through the "crisscrossing" of "types and styles of discourse" that Charles Bernstein describes in *Content's Dream*) has to be seen as only a preliminary step, a preparatory stage, not (as in Language poetry) as an end in itself.

We need Surrealism to remind us that language is not coextensive with the world—and that the world remakes itself in throes of convulsive beauty. Poetry ultimately needs to fall beyond words into things, becoming part of the abyssal aspect of things.

You spoke of the post-Surrealist or "critical" image as pointing in two directions at once: "it points back to itself as a linguistic construction within a world of associations, and it points outward to empirical referents in the world of things." But isn't this signpost in constant danger, in constant desire, of losing its own way? The Blakean cry "I want" is premised upon a body that cannot contain itself—upon language as the projection of an impossible body.

We now find ourselves in the second wave of response against the modernist ego-centered lyric, having learned much from the successes and defeats of the first wave. In my view, one of the most crippling defeats of the first wave was its failure to engage the sensorium—to activate the senses. This was the arena from which the traditional lyric drew much (even most) of its poetic power, yet the Language poets have failed to address themselves critically to the poetic activation of the body. For them, poetry has mostly remained a disembodied textual operation. Affective states are taken to be no more than signs, susceptible to metonymic manipulation like the rest.

(I have no intention of hypostasizing the body as some kind of "ultimate referent": it is necessarily a fraught and unstable entity, with perpetually shifting boundaries. Simply put, the body is that which is non-identical [and irreconcilable] to the text.)

The body is our closest star, our first and foremost reminder that there is something that escapes (it is not necessary to say "transcends") signification: it is our primary source of the Unsayable. The resistance to closure and totality, which you correctly cite as a property of the "critical image," can and should draw upon this primary source of the non-identical. In this way, the textual surface suddenly acquires a depth, a breadth, a breath. Despite their citations of Charles Olson, the Language poets have by and large neglected the Olsonian breath, of which Duncan remarked that it transports us immediately to a cosmological realm.

Duncan wrote: "We've to realize the cosmic intent or event that the physical body that we call 'ours' is 'an object which spontaneously or of its own order produces experience'; and that depth is 'asserted, or found out as such . . . implicit in physical being.' The thing is we have just this physical event we are, an incarnation, a body, a locality of cosmos having in that locality an experience of 'confronting' cosmos, in which our life, our experience of the actual, springs alive."

The "pointing toward the empirical" that you mention as one of the aspects of the critical image is, for me, nothing less than this first-order attentiveness to experience, which is inevitably the experience of incarnation. In our conversation in San Francisco, I compared the Language poets to Protestants fixated on the words of the text, and portrayed certain post-Surrealists as driven by an almost "Catholic" need to *activate and address the senses* (through the language-equivalents of stained glass, incense, etc.), taking the body as the site of the primary Mystery.

This irreducible mystery of the body corresponds to the mysterious body of language itself, which possesses its own materiality and momentum that cannot be reduced to its "social construction" (the Language poets' favorite explanatory paradigm). The mystery of language is that it "formed itself" behind our backs: its structure is not the result of intentionality or design. Language, in other words, was neither invented nor socially constructed. Like the body, it is a self-organizing cosmological system.

Language is an *emergent property* of social systems, just as organic life is an emergent property of inorganic matter ("emergence" being defined as a qualitative leap of matter beyond the laws of motion to which it previously conformed).

Language allows the animal to literally jump out of its skin— and to land inside a new and starkly paradoxical body.

These are the factors understood by the Surrealists, who developed the Romantic insight that meaning arises from an infinite and properly inexpressible depth. However, they all too readily identified this depth with the Freudian unconscious, whereas more recent (poststructuralist) investigations have revealed equally inexhaustible chasms occurring at every level of signification.

In the past century, poetic innovation has followed two divergent paths: experiential/sensual and formal/linguistic. The first path is represented by the tradition that extends from the Romantics to the Surrealists; the second by the Stein-Zukofsky-Language poetry axis. I think it is possible for "the critical image" to reunite these paths through a "new synthesis," an impossible rhetorical configuration capable of fusing metaphor (Surrealism) and metonymy (Language poetry).

Rather than the metaphorical assimilation of unlike to like:

$$A = B$$

Or the metonymic iteration of non-identity:

A ≠ A

This new rhetorical figure would instead tend to assume the shape of the German philosopher Schelling's maddening formulation:

$$(+A = B, A = B+) / A = A$$

where the idealist assertion of identity is mysteriously fractured by a function containing the promise of emergence marked by plus signs.

For this reason, I have found it necessary to rewrite Lautréamont's famous trope in the following way: "Against the operations of chance, it is sufficient to call upon the sign of the Umbrella, that which opens outward, or the Sewing Machine, that which stitches together—inasmuch as meaning will be defined systematically as a series of openings and closings upon the dissecting table of Language."

Every figure of speech, no matter how "poetic," recirculates meaning within a limited economy. And nothing can prevent this endless circulation of signs, apart from silence and paradox.

Silence, however, once again produces unity from multiplicity. It is a form of frozen music that cannot withstand the heat of *poiesis*. Instead, the site of emergence (or star formation) within the sign system must be a warring- or a trysting-place: the ROSE that is a SORE, an EROS of fatefully interlocked, yet irreconcilable opposites.

Here we can finally glimpse, pressing through the membrane of the sign, the features of the Unsignifiable itself.

A paradox is both an opening and a closing, a wound, a window on the surface of signs. Even as it bars the way to human understanding, it yields access to the non-anthropomorphic senses of the body of language.

(However, paradoxes cannot be invented, only discovered: they are *objectively* embedded in the matter of meaning. And to discover them, it is up to poets to become, as the British poet Peter Redgrove has demanded, "scientists of the strange.")

Charles, I will end here. I have offered you (as in the title of one of your poems) a "blank page already black." I wish I could accompany you on a walk to the Pont Mirabeau, to further discuss the images reflected in more-than-human waters.

A Season Later than Winter

[An empty spacesuit stands propped in a corner of the half-ruined Museum of Flight. This note was found clutched in its glove.]

While seeds survive the winter, the flower that disseminated them does not. Likewise, the mind that understands this, and disseminates these words, will not survive the winter.

The line extends itself, the circle stands still.

I want to insist that the cycle of the seasons does not constitute a natural life-cycle: the analogy between the fate of a living organism and the Earth's orbital oscillation fails at the boundary between biological and mechanical motion, on the day of the longest night.

The swing of the pendulum represents not propagation but merely alternation. Unlike the alternator, the propagator never returns to an initial position. Once that light *that inhabits* fails, it fails with finality.

No doubt, the progress of spring, summer, fall, and winter corresponds to the birth, growth, senescence, and death of the organism. But the organism dies even as the world-clock is reset to zero. Here, the analogy between creature and creation breaks down.

Once this discontinuity is revealed, the passage from winter to spring can no longer be taken for granted. It assumes the power of contingency, the possibility of nothingness to become anything at all.

Here, the imagination wants to construct a new season, one capable of mediating between darkness and light. But let us avoid all mystical or religious fabulation, and imagine this undiscovered season as occurring *within nature*, as perhaps restoring a missing piece of nature.

How can time accommodate this moment that comes after the end, before the beginning? Only by moving sideways, like a line of writing . . .

The Crisis of the Crystal

What is the situation of the object in contemporary poetry? The form of this question, posed by André Breton in 1934, might seem disingenuous today. What concerns us now is not the object in itself but the system of signifying practices responsible for its construction. Yet for Breton, the "crisis of the object" is precipitated at this very point, at the juncture between the word and the world. Here, signification is unfailingly surprised by an emergent reality, a surreality whose hazardous objectivity moves in advance of all language games. Something like a surrealist philosophy of nature is implied here, where nature (both human and non-human) is conceived as an inherently self-revolutionizing process—that is, as an autocatalytic system. The emergent object has the capacity to convulse or negate the very system that engendered it. In poetry, this object would manifest itself by means of an image powerful enough to overthrow conventionalized regimes, not only of thought, but of bodily sensation as well.

All citations of Clark Coolidge's *The Crystal Text* are from the 1995 Sun & Moon edition. The poem was first published in 1986 by The Figures.

No doubt the surrealist image, which was intended to violently reconcile perception and representation, can no longer revolutionize poetic language. At present, representation has gained the upper hand over perception; the content of the sensorium, to the extent that it is meaningful, is held to be "always already" structured by discourse. Today, the perception of strange and unprecedented phenomena, once facilitated by poetry, is pursued instead by revolutionary science, most recently in studies of the nonlinear dynamics of complex systems. Meanwhile contemporary poetry, preoccupied by a concern for textuality, has largely lost sight of the ontologically disruptive object, along with most of the frenzies, delights, and paradoxes of sense-perception.

In light of these developments, how is one to construe the object at the center of Clark Coolidge's poem *The Crystal Text*? The object is, in fact, a crystal, a naturally occurring substance. An object that humans, in imitation of nature, have learned to produce but that owes none of its defining features—its stability, for example, or its symmetry—to human design. Coolidge, in the course of a book-length poetic contemplation of this object, discovers that the crystal itself is empty and still, that it can be filled and animated only by its reflections and refractions of human experience. In this poem, the natural object provokes memory and reverie. But Coolidge emphasizes that the crystal itself "cannot speak" (107). That is, nature without human presence is a deserted stage, a desert, as Kant declared, along with many other thinkers of the Enlightenment (Diderot remarked in the Encyclopedia that "it is the presence of humans that makes the existence of things interesting"). Likewise, in Coolidge's poem, the crystal "does nothing" (116); it seems to contain the light of experience, but remains "notionless of its fill"

(111). Coolidge comes to realize that "What you see is only what you put there" (93). By treating mind as active subject and nature as passive object, Coolidge's work appears, at first glance, to be inscribed within some version of idealism.

Coolidge's long dialogue with the unanswering crystal is effectively a monologue, a day-book of the poet's frustrated attempts to communicate with "the stone." The apparent failure of this procedure would seem to confirm a scientific understanding of the crystal, and of nature in general, as a cold mechanical system, indifferent to human supplication. However, Coolidge's approach to the stone is anything but scientific. For him, the crystal becomes a magic mirror that transforms the questioner's own visage into an oracular mask, mouthing riddles and giving back the questions themselves as mirror-reversed answers.

Coolidge's poem thus participates in the prescientific tradition of crystal-gazing, of "scrying," as the practice was called by Renaissance *magi*. In this tradition, the scryer would retire, as Coolidge does, to a quiet room to consult the crystal. Beforehand the crystal would have been magically charged by a series of ritual incantations known as "the Call." The passages of poetic improvisation with which Coolidge frames his own questioning of the crystal similarly accelerate meaning, lending a polysemous "charge" to the object at the focus of the text. Finally, the scryer would fine-tune the sensitivity of the crystal through methods of astrological and numerological positioning. Coolidge also is alert to occult correspondences—as, for example, when he observes that "There are 13 letters to my name . . . There are 13 facets to this crystal" (99, 100).

Unlike the Renaissance *magi*, however, Coolidge is not interested in using the crystal as a means of clairvoyance. He pursues only the traces of his own presence among the crystal's baffling lights and silences. Because the crystal refuses the petitions of its scryer-poet, all his accounts of the stone's interior inevitably become self-reflexive. To keep a record of crystal-gazing is, as Coolidge states, "To write / a long book of nothing 'but looking deeply into oneself'" (12). But this is a prospect, he adds, to be greeted with "a laugh. / A scorn, not for oneself probably but for the possibility of a self view" (12).

In this passage, Coolidge compares the self to a mirror that, as a "reflecting surface," is incapable of reflecting its own image. As Coolidge confesses, "I dived at you, self, but you rubbed me blank / in all my own mirrors" (12). Writing of the crystal's emptiness, then, bears a strong similarity to writing of the self's own emptiness: "The crystal attains toward a transparency / my mirror approaches, face or no face" (13). At the same time, crystal and self mirror each other's emptiness within the "reflecting surface" of writing; as Coolidge states, "Writing is all reflections. And said reflection's stilled / connections" (115).

The self, the stone, and writing all appear to be faces of the same crystal: a diagram of their relation would form a triangle, the most basic of linear planes. The play of light in *The Crystal Text* is conditioned by the self-reflection of this triangular plane as it rotates through various configurations: "I crystallized myself out of flesh / but this is wrong. I learned to scratch / down words on paper by tendency of crystal / adjacent to sleeping area" (37). Later, Coolidge compares the written page to a facet of crystal: "Writing on the side of a page, a wall / in a world of inter-bladed and filtering walls" (47).

If writing is "all reflections," then the system of writing can never reflect itself. The true face of writing appears as the vanishing point at the center of a self-reflecting mirror. Consequently, Coolidge writes, "The text of crystal might / reveal everything but itself" (79). Musing on strategies of writing, Coolidge remarks that "One could divide it all up into / those who know how the work should be / and those who never know before the work" (33). Those writers "who never know before the work" are undoubtedly poets; after all, Coolidge asks, "How much poetry is unprovoked thought?" (27). Consulting the stone in this regard, he announces: "As the crystal says, speech without blindness is worth little" (84). The work must take shape blindly but surely, in accordance with a process that resembles crystal growth: "It fascinates me now to see if I find things to speak what shapes their sentences will take" (29). But even as the poet attempts to "find things to speak," he also finds that "The crystal cannot speak. The good book cannot speak" (107). At one point, the poet, "[b]ending over the crystal . . . wonder[ing] what writing would proceed," exclaims, "If only speech could talk" (42).

Coolidge's meditations on the inability of a reflecting surface to reflect itself seem to recapitulate the theories of the nineteenth-century mathematician Georg Cantor on the paradoxes of self-referential sets. In 1895, Cantor asked a question that remains unanswerable in terms of ordinary logic: Is a set that is composed of all possible sets to be counted as a member of itself? If not, then the set fails to correspond to its own definition. If so, then the set chases its own tail by becoming a number larger than itself. Here, Coolidge's doubts about "the possibility of a self view" are confirmed by the Hegelian philosopher Howard Kainz, who considers that

"self-consciousness *is* that class which is a member of itself."[1]
Neither the self nor its "text of crystal" can adequately reflect
itself without falling into contradiction and, ultimately, si-
lence. Looking into the crystal, Coolidge asks, "Is the heart
of poetry a stillness?" (150).

Coolidge's question finds some precedent not only in logical,
but also in linguistic theory. For example, structuralism pos-
its a crystalline stillness within language, analyzing the rela-
tion between signifier and signified as a series of "stilled con-
nections." As the hermeneutic philosopher Manfred Frank
points out, in Saussure's structural theory of language "one
and only one signified is assigned to every signifier. This,
moreover, occurs according to a form and lasting rule that
allows both the differentiation of signs and their recombina-
tion . . . call[ing] to mind the image of a crystal lattice." Frank
goes on to observe that "In a crystal lattice the molecules are
not only distinct from one another, they are, at a constant
low temperature, *fixed to their places*; i.e., they cannot swarm
outward, nor is there any blurring that would make their lo-
cation and thus their application uncontrollable."[2]

Yet for Coolidge the appearance of "stillness" is imposed
by the paradoxes of self-reflexivity, not by the fixity of the
connection between signifier and signified. Such fixity can
be attributed only to a closed and stable structure, whereas
Coolidge's text of crystal fails to either enclose or stabilize its
own reflection. Furthermore, its "stilled connections" con-

1. Howard P. Kainz, *Paradox, Dialectic, and System* (University Park: Penn-
sylvania State University Press, 1988), p. 26.
2. Manfred Frank, *What Is Neostructuralism?* (Minneapolis: University of
Minnesota Press, 1989), pp. 23–24.

ceal another paradox: as the poet discovers, "Movement is the hidden / apex of the stillness / the crystal tends" (128). Here, fixity of structure is "collapsed in a calypso of eclipses" (62), a play of light and shadow that multiplies in all directions without benefit of a centralizing "self view." Thus, "there is something missing from it [the text]: a center which arrests and grounds the play of substitutions."[3] All the same, the work of Coolidge does not entirely corroborate the poststructuralist critique of centered, stabilized meaning. The moment of divergence is obvious: the depiction of language as a crystal, an idea supposedly shattered by poststructuralism, persists in Coolidge's poem.

The poet claims to be writing, or growing, a "text of crystal." And, as Coolidge acknowledges, "The crystal is a problem of structure" (142). But in what way is the structure of Coolidge's writing crystalline? Even as its paradoxes of self-reflection empty into silence, *The Crystal Text* continues to be filled with noise: with anecdotes, scraps of other texts, desultory notes, diary entries. The texture of the text—at once improvisatory and coolly detached, a kind of "writing without thinking" (115)—resembles the random swirls of atoms in liquid or in glass (a supercooled liquid) far more than it does the orderly rows of atoms in a crystal.

Nonetheless, Coolidge insists that "The window glass is but a gross imitation of the crystal, as speech is of poetry" (107). Here, the "glass" of speech is asserted to be an *imitation*—a poor reflection—of the "crystal" of poetry. In other words, the glassy disorder of speech is held to *derive from*—even as it distorts—the higher, crystalline order of poetry. For Coolidge,

3. Jacques Derrida, *Writing and Difference*, trans. Alan Bass (Chicago: University of Chicago Press, 1978), p. 289.

it seems, ordinary language is merely the projection into our three-dimensional universe of a higher-dimensional language, the language of *The Crystal Text*. Since we cannot visualize higher dimensions, we may find this order of language is inaccessible ("Poetry is the closed voice?" [107]), but at least its reflection, its "gross imitation," is evident in everyday speech. The tangled vernacular of Coolidge's lines turns out to be a cross-section of an elegantly structured hyperspace crystal.

Strangely enough, just one year after Coolidge completed his poem, researchers in a government laboratory discovered an "impossible" crystal requiring a theory of higher dimensions to explain it. In 1984 at the National Bureau of Standards, a metallic alloy was first melted, then rapidly cooled to produce a substance that paradoxically combines the amorphousness of glass with the interlocking structure of crystal. The atomic lattices of this new substance, dubbed a "quasicrystal," fit together as perfectly as those of an ordinary crystal. But the arrangements of quasicrystalline lattices do not repeat in the usual crystalline manner. Instead, such perfectly fitted, yet nonperiodic patterns appear orderly only when viewed as the projection of an abstract, higher-dimensional lattice.[4] Of course, this picture provides only a mathematical, not a physical, explanation. As one scientist confessed, "no one could think of a mechanism by which millions upon millions of real atoms could arrange themselves spontaneously in those intricate patterns."[5] Most attempts at physical explanations have involved a theory of tiled surfaces. That theory, formulated by the mathematician Roger Penrose ten

4. Peter W. Stephens and Alan I. Goldman, "The Structure of Quasicrystals," *Scientific American* 264, no. 2 (April 1991): 46–47.

5. Hans C. von Baeyer, "Impossible Crystals," *Discover* 11, no. 2 (Feb. 1990): 76.

years before the discovery of quasicrystals, solves the problem of how to cover a surface completely with sets of tiles whose patterns do not repeat periodically. To ensure nonperiodicity, Penrose developed specific rules for fitting the tiles together, rules that govern both local and global features of the resulting pattern. But the blind workings of nature must act locally and cannot think globally. As one scientist put it, "Local rules for adding tiles are analogous to forces that attract and hold new atoms to the surface of a growing quasicrystal; they are plausible ingredients in the growth mechanism. Global rules are not. The atoms on a growing surface do not plan ahead. They respond only to the interatomic sticking force of their immediate neighbors. If quasiperiodic patterns could be constructed only with the help of global rules, they could not be assembled by real atoms."[6] So far, this contradiction remains unresolved: the locally applicable laws for fitting the parts together are not sufficient to generate the whole pattern.

This contradiction manifests itself also in the "impossible" crystal of Coolidge's text. As Coolidge observes, "There is no overview but in/the strictly local system. . . . Back to the thought, the crystal/open while closed" (27). The structure of *The Crystal Text*, since it permits only a local rather than a global view, would seem to have more in common with that of a quasicrystal than with that of an ordinary crystal. This talisman of the self and of writing is "open while closed": open because "now we have no method and the crystal is as clear as unmixed air" (118), closed because the principle of its making, its *poiesis*, remains inaccessible and perhaps unknowable.

As Coolidge testifies, "Perspective lies, the/universe has no one comprehensible form" (81). This he demonstrates by pre-

6. Ibid., pp. 76–77.

senting an object that he himself defines as a locally inter-
acting, non-globalizable system, one that cannot reflect itself
as a totality. If the overall pattern of a system is determined,
not by system-wide but by local interactions, and if none of
these local interactions reflects the pattern of the system as a
whole, then the behavior of that system fractures the mirror
of cause and effect and becomes *nonlinear*: "Words that are
shavings off the irreducible block. / Words that remain the
elegance at Chaos Gate" (62). The defining feature of such
complex systems, according to systems theorist Niklas Luh-
mann, is that they contain more possibilities than can be ac-
tualized.[7] Coolidge concurs: "The crystal is but one nexus in
the drain / of speeded possibles" (94).

Not all unrealized possibilities, however, hold the promise of
revolutionary change. Many nonlinear or chaotic systems (a
swinging pendulum, for example) cycle through endless vari-
ations, none of which need alter the character of the system
itself. In many cases, the behavior of a nonlinear dynamical
system is locally unpredictable, but globally stable. This is
true of the formation of quasicrystals; is it true of Coolidge's
text as well? In the citation above, the "words" derive from
an "irreducible block," a state that implies stability. Coolidge
further says, "It is perfect of imperfection. / The most perfect
field a surfeit / of randomly bounding objects" (90). Now, in
the vocabulary of nonlinear dynamics, a map of all possible
states of a given system is called the "phase space" of that sys-
tem. The phase space of *The Crystal Text*, then, seems to be
represented by a globally stable "most perfect field" that con-
tains a locally unpredictable "surfeit / of randomly bounding
objects."

7. Cited in Paul Cilliers, *Complexity and Postmodernism* (London: Rout-
ledge, 1998), p. 2.

However, as the philosopher Manuel De Landa points out, "since phase spaces (by definition) include *all the possible states* for a given system, it follows that (by definition) no truly novel states can be represented by phase spaces."[8] The emergence of truly novel properties within a system disrupts or even eradicates the topology of its phase space. For example, the emergence of living systems disrupts the phase space of chemical reactions governed by entropic flows, just as the emergence of language bursts the topology of instinctive social behavior.

A revolutionary rupture of this order constitutes the "crisis of the object," as the surrealists understood it. The surrealist object materializes (at) this unprecedented—and therefore fantastic—moment of rupture. In contrast, Coolidge's object conserves reality. The crystal remains a crystal, a field of reference within which everyday experiences randomly rebound. The transcendental emptiness of the crystal—and ultimately, of signification itself—defeats the senses and turns the mind back upon itself in an infinitely reflexive recession.

How is this different from Breton's declaration that surrealism seeks "the annihilation of being into a diamond"? First, Coolidge insists on the *textuality* of the object, while Breton insists on its inescapable *materiality*. Furthermore, the textuality of Coolidge's work leads to the object's dematerialization, while Breton's commitment to materiality recognizes the object's emergence from elsewhere (namely, the realm of the marvelous). Unlike the poetics of textuality, surrealist poetics shares the conviction of Enlightenment science that sense-perception has the power to overthrow the structures of the mind.

8. Manuel De Landa, *A Thousand Years of Nonlinear History* (New York: Zone Books, 1997), p. 277.

THE CRY AT ZERO

Masked Dialectic

Forced witness. That the face of witnessing become, finally, its own slashed portrait.

The details vanish, not forgotten but subsumed. An everyday occurrence raised on its hind legs, crazed by lightning.

Walls worn smooth by those who have passed here. The story of civilization is screened nightly.

In proximity of a ribcage enclosing clockwork, the head fairly swims with sentiment.

Further tragedies exist beyond motion. A glyph is also a coagulum, drawing blackness from the white crevices of time.

Ceased continues, spectral within *seized*. The raw cords are replaced by silvery trails of fluid.

Plotted against these coordinates, the noise of sunrise: a thought empinnacled on hierarchy's ruin.

On Alexandrian Philosophy

[introduction to Will Alexander's Towards the Primeval Lightning Field*]*

1

Primeval: the undifferentiated.

Lightning: the differential stroke itself.

There are many ways to contemplate the world, but only one way to change it: to steal the fire of its birth.

All that is reflected is not created. All that is not reflected is created.

The mirror's First Philosophy: a crucible of molten sand.

2

This is a book of First Philosophy.

Whose *telos* is not the reconstruction of knowledge, but its (necessarily furious) production.

Offering not a system of the world, but a frame for its Originary Furor, or Furnace.

For the self-evidence of why there is something rather than nothing.

3

First Philosophy is (according to Aristotle, who introduced the term) the science of being *qua* being.

. Of the primary and therefore primeval attributes of being.

But Alexander is not the student of Aristotle.

The "primeval," for Aristotle, is that which *exists always and already* without having been created. What is uncreated, and so unconditioned by any force of change, must be perfectly changeless, and therefore motionless. All motion is only a striving to attain—to return to—this supreme state of motionlessness. What is uncreated creates, what is motionless causes motion, only by remaining absolutely still: by its very simplicity and perfection, *it is the ultimate object of desire*, and so arouses and provokes the potential to become actual.

There is an ontological rupture here, between the uncreated and the created, which can be overcome only by invoking the mythological power of *eros*. What other power is capable of reconciling timelessness and time?

Aristotle's Prime Mover (who would later be rehabilitated as the God of Aquinas) thus holds out the promise of rest to the restless: in other words, the metaphysics of eternity must banish the physics of infinity. For, as Aristotle argues in Book XII of the *Metaphysics*, a physical infinity of causes can neither lead to, nor derive from, a state of absolute equilibrium or perfection.

Now, Alexander's First Philosophy is also concerned with the generation of the world. Yet Alexander's *genetrix*, unlike Aristotle's, itself is caught up in the flux of change, and does not stand ontologically apart from it. Nonetheless, for both thinkers, generation is necessitated by the primary attribute of being. In Aristotle's case, it is an "eternal actuality" (toward which all potentiality strives); in Alexander's case, it is an "infinite potentiality" (from which all actuality proceeds).

The mirror-symmetry is clear: the place filled by the "uncreated" in Aristotle's system is occupied by the "inexhaustible" in Alexander's. So that absolute equilibrium, for Alexander, must be equivalent to *thanatos*. A perfect state of rest cannot contain desire: faced with the lightning-storm of Alexander's thought, the changeless self-sufficiency of Aristotle's "uncreated" being is revealed to be finally indistinguishable from nothingness.

As Aristotle himself testifies, eternity is surrounded by lightning, and can have no other consequence than lightning. (In the words of the French poet René Char, "Though we inhabit a flash of lightning, it is the heart of the eternal.") If, as Aristotle argues, motionlessness radiates motion by means of *eros*, Alexander shows that radiative *eros* therefore assumes the power of a first principle (even if it is the outer shell of nothingness).

4

If motion ("lightning") has ontological priority over motionlessness (the "uncreated"), then motion cannot rest absolutely within its own state of being-in-motion. Yet what motion could encompass (and therefore overtake) the process of change itself? One answer is suggested by Alexander's use of the modifier "primeval" in relation to "lightning."

The primeval moment is privileged to the degree that it occurs *in advance* of all other moments. In relation to what follows, its position in time is not contingent, but necessary. For a sequence of time that lacked a first moment would be equivalent to an eternity.

In eternity, each moment is equal to every other, and by this equivalence, all moments are reduced to one: to the instantaneousness of lightning, the "heart of the eternal." To condition "lightning"—this timeless singularity, this pure noun produced by the stilling of a verb—with the modifier "primeval" is to assert that one is not equal to itself, and therefore to posit a unique moment of crisis within eternity. The moment of self-division, of emergence, must always be an emergency.

The frame of Alexander's philosophy is the collapsing structure of eternity. Yet it is this "field" that offers resistance to the birth of time. This ghostly integument is to be burst asunder.

It happens, literally, in "no time." By definition, there can be no narrative, no series of causes, antecedent to this event: after the hush of negation, the splitting of the sky is unprecedented.

The lightning-stroke is an inscription, a natural hieroglyph that conveys the message: *Eternity has already happened.*

So that, in an important sense, Alexander's philosophy begins at the end. Or more precisely, *after* the end, *before* the beginning. Now—at this strange juncture between time and timelessness—comes to pass the Emergency of Emergence. In which everything presents itself at once, as an event that, containing all other events, therefore cannot contain itself.

Where Occidental thought has tended to reconstruct the world starting from its smallest units, or, as in Descartes' *Meditations on First Philosophy,* from a minimum number of "clear and distinct ideas," Alexander's method takes as irreducibly "given" only what is largest, most indistinct and undifferentiated: Universal History as an instantaneous burst of information.

The idea of such an information burst—a Signal composed of the sum total of all signals—has been proposed at least once before, not in a philosophical work, but in a short story by James Blish entitled "Beep" (first published in 1954 in a pulp science-fiction magazine).

In this story, Blish describes the invention of a device called "the Dirac communicator" that can send and receive messages at "*any* distance, instantaneously." The device works by collapsing information into a "Dirac pulse." Somewhat ironically, the device registers this pulse as a "small *beep* of sound"; each message thus appears to correspond to its own distinctive beep. However, as Blish's protagonist explains,

Every Dirac message that is sent is picked up by every receiver that is capable of receiving it. *Every* receiver—including the first one ever built, through the hundreds of thousands of them which will exist throughout the Galaxy in the twenty-fourth century, to the untold millions which will exist in the thirtieth century, and so on. The Dirac beep is the simultaneous reception of *every one of the Dirac messages which has ever been sent, or ever will be sent.*

In the course of the story, the inventors learn how to "slow down" the playback of this instantaneous Signal of signals in order to read the individual messages contained within it.

Likewise, every one of Alexander's surrational propositions has the quality of a slowed-down Dirac beep. (The "beep" also bears a strong similarity to André Breton's "supreme point," wherein all contradictions between past and future, known and unknown, life and death, are reconciled.)

Alexander's propositional "pulse" begins at the end: with the assumption that a totality of meanings is realized immediately within the lightning-signal. The philosopher-poet's task, then, is to decelerate this instantaneous burst, so that its contents may enter into Language.

Alexander's methodology here is neither deductive nor inductive, but *con*ductive. Thesis passes into antithesis with electric fluidity, never terminating in synthesis: the relationship between statements (as in a Dirac transmission) is non-hierarchical and non-cumulative.

The prodigality of the lightning-strike demands a like extravagance in the language employed, not only to describe this Ur-phenomenon, but to conceive and embody it. "Primeval lightning" seeks the sign of a *free expenditure* that, as Bataille has shown, must transgress the boundaries of all restricted economies of meaning. Hence Alexander's aggressively transgressive use of language: the neologisms, archaisms, and etymological dislocations; the focus throws between denotation and connotation; the radical recontextualization of specialized vocabularies.

In the essay "Language Leap as Inscrutable Physic," Alexander contemplates "language near its origin," as "alchemic fulcrum." For words too must be understood under the sign of the Emergency of Emergence. The more closely the moment of origin is approached, the more things start to resemble one another, and to overflow their conventionally assigned boundaries.

It is at this point, when mirrors turn molten, that reflection proves equal to creation.

5

In this work, there is no generic discontinuity between philosophy and poetry. Indeed, the book in hand might have been subtitled *Against Discontinuity*, or perhaps *Against Exilic Abstraction*: for its whole argument consists of making resoundingly concrete connections (via lightning and other conceptual leaps) between an encyclopedic array of facts and figures (the "information burst").

Against the "linear Babels" of alienated discourses, Alexander argues for "a new perpendicular burst, transmuting in demeanour," for a language in which the vocabularies of magic and science become (once again, but as never before) interchangeable.

This "unified theory" of science and magic appears to consummate the unfinished project of Renaissance philosophy (cut short by the rise of the mechanical worldview in alliance with capitalism). Of course, Alexander's open-ended dynamical universe hardly resembles the static Renaissance conception of nature. Yet he shares a great affinity with the scientist-magicians of that era; his strategies of textual recombination are prefigured especially by the work of the sixteenth-century *magus* Giordano Bruno.

Bruno inscribed—just as Alexander does here—a version of magical animism upon the classical texts of scientific materialism. According to the historian Frances Yates, "Bruno found the conceptions of infinite space and innumerable worlds in Lucretius' *De natura rerum*. But he absolutely transforms the Lucretian notions by imparting to the innumerable worlds magical animation, totally absent from Lucretius' cold universe." And just as Bruno has appropriated the discourse of ancient atomism for Hermetic ends, Alexander draws upon the latest scientific findings for the purpose of "join[ing] forces with the Great Work, with the hallucinatory beatitudes of magic." In the work of both poet-philosophers, the "cold universe" of science is *aufgehoben*: at once cancelled and raised to a higher level of imaginal fire.

As Yates points out, "the imagination . . . was Bruno's chief magical method." For him, its potency far exceeded the more widely recognized methods that rely upon the manipulation of talismanic objects. The "magically animated imagination [was] 'the sole gate to all internal affections and the link of links.' Bruno's language is excited and obscure," Yates continues, "as he expounds this, to him, central mystery, the conditioning of the imagination in such a way as to draw into the personality spiritual or demonic forces which will unlock its inner powers."

This pre-Romantic idea of the imagination as "the link of links" still dwells in the thought and practice of Alexander. Here, the energy of the imagination has not yet been harnessed (as it would be in Romanticism) to the goals of bourgeois subjectivization. It can never be a matter of "possessing" this imagination, but only (as in the communalistic spirit of *voudou*) of being possessed by it. Imagination is the conductor of primeval lightning, the fiery trickster leaping between frozen and fragmented *realia*, the universal translator of the multitude of tongues (both human and Inhuman) emitted by the Signal of signals.

The Alexandrian imagination is a compendium of Brunian links, an infinite library of "lucid catacombs and spirals."

After the conquests of Alexander, a city was founded in his name on the northern coast of Africa. There, in the third century BCE, the world's first universal library was built, a storehouse (in its metaphysical form, at least) of all the books that had ever been written and that ever would be written. The First Philosophy of Alexander is situated exactly here, at the intersection of the African, Asian, and European landmasses.

The library was destroyed by fire and rebuilt, only to be destroyed again. (The fire itself was stolen and returned to these writings, only to be stolen again.) Within the form of this book, the Library of Alexandria is still burning.

The Removes

After the Time Epidemic, the eyes of owls were found embedded throughout the soft balustrades, reminders of—

A fateful plan your cellmates (in this centuries-wide prison, whose actual walls have yet to be discovered) will soon deploy against you—

This is understandable. You are waiting to achieve your paradigm, a damaged star. Running like smoke from the Chamber of Ills, your signature commences—

"Against the operations of chance," you write, "it is sufficient to call upon the sign of the Umbrella, that which opens outward, or the Sewing Machine, that which stitches together—inasmuch as meaning will be defined systematically as a series of openings and closings upon the dissecting table of Language."

Thus, the words of your confession appear as vestiges of an

Original speechlessness, ragged holes in the firmament—

"What phoneme in integers is also present in jewels?"—Why answer? The laws of thermodynamics can't forgive you because your name is a darkened festival of sound.

Here, then, is the gift of your exhaustion—a precious animal stroked to transparency.

Here, too, is a windowless sunset—its proof scratched out by the charred branches of your eyes.

Your pursuers, inevitable, still trust in the parallelism of acts where desires converge. Yet space itself must be spoken aloud, the emanation of a veil . . .

Pink Noise

Logic is a space without shadows, a space whose objective necessity nonetheless is haunted by the absence of a (freely acting) subject. Likewise, a formal poem, one whose unfolding is determined strictly by rules, often retains a sense of mystery, the feeling of an abandoned, yet somehow still actively functioning world.

With scarce any grounds for settled conviction,
light slipping on animated surface slides its stars

into the eye of a storm where regions of calm
embrace, divide in sleep to write:
words repel each other, each seeking isolation,
pass the threshold into the palaces of our instructors.

Mary Margaret Sloan's long poem "On Method" (versions of which now have appeared in the periodicals *Abacus* and *Chain*) stands as an exemplar of a postmodern text haunted by its own formalism, whose rule-laden self-generation hides a mystery at its heart—the mystery to which pure logic itself is subordinated.

To paraphrase Gödel: No system of rules can produce a poem unless that system *also* allows words to relate in ways that exceed guidance by the system.

"On Method," as Sloan states in her preface to the poem, "began as a reading of Descartes' *Discourse on Method*." Sloan explains that she wished to "escape" both the "boredom" of free forms and traditional forms: "I wanted the poem to involve a method that would explore a classical model of order with a mathematical basis and would then wreck itself from within, deteriorate that classical symmetry and develop as a complex adaptive system into a more flexible model of order . . . I wanted a procedure that would permit exploration of the pleasures of restraint, in particular, of mathematical restraint."

Remote light shattered at our feet in the optical
palace, interior walls, as always, painted dead black in
order to prevent internal reflections.

Sloan's "On Method" is a poem conditioned, but not controlled, by the application of rules. Indeed, tension between the method and its poetic *dépassement* is one of this work's most compelling features. In poiesis (as opposed to verbal game-playing), words are arranged more or less methodically, but only in order to go beyond words, to say the unsayable.

At the same time, there can be no poetry without constraints. Language is the most complex medium available to any artist; it is never given in a "pure" state, but arrives (always, already) layered and overdetermined by conventions and formalizations of every kind. A poem inevitably must be played upon the interwoven strings of these language-constraining systems.

In the case of "On Method," an explicitly artificial system of rules overrides and filters "natural" language protocols, creating a clearing, an *elsewhere*. As the poem slowly builds and recycles in accordance with Sloan's formalism, the experience of reading acquires a trance-like quality similar to the experience of viewing Alain Resnais's film *Last Year at Marienbad* (a work whose mystery likewise depends on the unfolding of a formal pattern). In Sloan's poem, we "pass the threshold into the palace of our instructors"—that is, into an architext replete with formal devices—just as in Resnais's film, the protagonists become caught in a complex temporal loop and wander through the endless corridors of a castle. Both works play out as inexorable rituals set among relics of classical reason.

We must do the same, apparently, perish
rather than delay, astonished, as mathematical
foundations yield no graceful superstructure, while
artful moral palaces built on sand and mud

are informed by reasonable error. As if looking
were reversed, our guide made signs, none of us
understanding accuracies of reflection.

The formalism of "On Method," as Sloan indicates in her preface, is designed to "wreck itself from within." Her work thereby alludes to and allegorizes those developments in logic and mathematics that, since the end of the nineteenth century, have shaken the foundations of classical reason (viz. Riemann's discovery of non-Euclidean geometries, Cantor's discovery of irresolvable paradoxes in number theory, and Gödel's discovery of axiomatic incompleteness).

However, the specific formalism that Sloan has chosen—a rondel whose repeating lines increase in length (i.e., number of words) according to an algebraic function—never abandons the classical confines of the Cartesian coordinate system. While the arrangement of words within the poem is made to undergo a "mathematically determined deterioration," the mathematical model itself maintains its stability in relation to "a central Cartesian axis."

Moreover, the uncanny lyricism of this work cannot be attributed entirely to its mathematical method, since the method does not pertain to word choice. Yet the semantic surface of the text shares the paradoxical, counter-intuitive, and non-formalizable qualities of post-Cartesian mathematics, even as the poem's deep structure conserves the "clear and distinct" ideals of Cartesian method. Here, formal constraint serves as a propaedeutic for the poetic imagination, which in the end is driven by inspiration rather than rules.

If the middle ground is a middle term, site of exclusion,
then, after penetrating the sacred grounds disguised,
we gave our animals into the hands, extremities,
of the observers. Theirs was a still-born range

where as colors of the sky evaporated, lack
remained, replacing vision. Simple and unmagnified, stars,
keeping their distance and details intact,
shower the crystalline lens. Transubstantiation
of sentience to a circle of masonry,

the palace, in which were propped apertures
in diversity. Our guide motioned us from within to
inspect the place of which so many
species of memory were made.

Indeed, Sloan's language may be most "mathematical" when it is most inspired: for we are living in an era—though few seem to realize it—of the convergence of science, mathematics, and poetry. Christopher Langton, a leading researcher in the science of complex systems, has said that the understanding of nonlinear interactions can be enhanced by poetic thought: "Poetry is a very nonlinear use of language, where the meaning is more than just the sum of the parts. I have the feeling that culturally there's going to be something like poetry in the future of science" (*Scientific American*, June 1995).

Even in the mid-nineteenth century, as cracks were beginning to appear in the foundations of reason, the German mathematician Karl Weierstrass observed that "A mathematician who is not also something of a poet will never be a perfect mathematician."

Weierstrass is credited with the discovery of the first fractal object—a curve consisting completely of corners (that is, every corner is made up of further corners *ad infinitum*). Such a curve occupies more space than a one-dimensional line, but occupies less space than a two-dimensional circle or square. Its dimensionality is fractional, thus prompting the descriptive term *fractal*. Subsequently, many more patterns exhibiting fractal self-similarity have been discovered both in mathematics and in nature.

By the mid-twentieth century, the Polish mathematician Benoit Mandelbrot had discovered an extraordinarily intricate class of fractals based on complex numbers (i.e., numbers generated by the square roots of negative numbers). Patterns produced by the Mandelbrot set are highly nonlinear, bifurcating chaotically while remaining self-similar at all scales.

In her preface to "On Method," Sloan reveals that, in composing the poem, "Initially I tried using a fractal model but couldn't discover a repeatable prosodic unit that would lend itself to a suitable rate of growth based on a fractal ratio; in relation to the countable elements of a poem (syllables, words per line, lines, and so on), the rate of growth was too rapid to be felt."

It is understandable that poets who seek to infuse language with the counter-intuitive and vertiginous properties of post-Cartesian mathematics might be tempted to adopt a fractal-based method of writing. The Mandelbrot set, however, is spectacularly unsuited to such procedures, mainly because the square roots of negative numbers have no counterparts in the world of physical objects (including linguistic objects such as letters, words, lines of verse, or stanzas). It is true that complex numbers can be represented geometrically as points, but the points cannot be located on a standard coordinate grid of whole numbers. Instead, they must be displayed on a modified grid called the Argand plane, where imaginary and real numbers intersect. However, no part of language can be made to correspond—without violence—to this dizzyingly abstract intersection. (Leibniz referred to complex numbers as a "sublime outlet of the divine spirit, an amphibian between being and not-being"; Euler deemed them to be not only imaginary, but "impossible" numbers.)

Still, not all fractals derive from complex numbers or exhibit chaotic patterns. Such "linear" fractals may prove more amenable to linkage with systems of language. An example is provided by the "Sierpinski gasket," constructed by inscribing an inverted equilateral triangle inside another equilateral triangle (so that the apex of the inner triangle touches the base of the outer one). This means that the enclosed area on each side of the inverted triangle also becomes a triangle. The procedure is repeated for each successively appearing triangle ad infinitum. The resulting pattern, despite its simplicity, possesses the primary feature of fractal entities: self-similarity at all scales (i.e., each part is identical to the whole).

Thanks to L.S.D. (Littérature Semi-Définitionnelle), a project undertaken by French writers Marcel Bénabou and Georges Perec, we can cite a writing procedure analogous to the Sierpinski gasket. Take a sheet of lined paper; write one word on the first line; on the next line, write the definition of that word; on the next, the definitions of each word of the preceding definition; and so on. The result is an expansion of the meaning of one word, comparable to the numeric expansion of Pascal's Triangle (a stack of numbers in which any number is the sum of the two numbers situated immediately above it). Furthermore, it can be demonstrated that Pascal's Triangle is an arithmetic version of the Sierpinski gasket.

Bénabou and Perec later became founding members of Oulipo (Ouvroir de Littérature Potentielle), a French movement devoted to the use of formal procedures in literary writing. Formulated in opposition to surrealist methods of automatic writing, the Oulipians' "bon usage de la contrainte" nonetheless similarly strives to free literature from the domination of conscious intentionality and to allow literary language somehow to construct itself.

Mary Margaret Sloan, as the author of "On Method," now must be considered the foremost *oulipienne américaine*. Perhaps we have not yet arrived at the point, to paraphrase Weierstrass, where "a poet who is not also something of a mathematician will never be a perfect poet," but at least an idea may be dawning on poets that language is capable of levels of organization far beyond personal, or even social, experience. Mathematics offers a significant means of accessing these levels.

As Sloan implies in her preface, post-personal poetic language must "develop as a complex adaptive system," poised on the cusp between order and chaos, between the "white noise" of utter randomness and the "brown noise" of repetitive-signal transmission. The zone in which surprising information can be transmitted is termed "pink noise," and it is precisely toward this interzone that Sloan has adjusted the modulation of her marvelous device.

First Drift

If we cannot be anything other than imperfect, a little tired, saddened, or distracted by those things we do not recognize (and familiar because of that)—

If we cannot be anything other than this—disquieted by the slowest possible music, yet listening intently—

Truth is reductive. Therefore, attend to those ideas whose boundaries lack edges, whose tones are just beginning to be infiltrated by disbelief. Allow your body to become a warped effect of that knowledge, a bow drawn backward across the strings—

Toward a blue identity resembling, although not possessing, the roundness of pain.

An excessive chord indwelling, proliferating tendrils, deemed by Lovecraft the *Crawling Chaos*—that which the insomniac writer E. M. Cioran called a "pandemonium of paradoxical symmetries."

To understand the veiled sound of the viol, study the curtains of light that surround extinguished suns.

—In medieval Arabic mathematics, such curvatures reach down to noise; a series of pictures invalidated by the doctrine of the motionless traveler.

We also (wanting elision) recorded the simultaneities' lateness. The round window laid horizontal: a zero. "We," meaning: many other figures of glass, collected at right angles.— Intense repose.

Wine + Hashish

The decadent poet George Sterling committed suicide by swallowing a cyanide capsule in his room at the Bohemian Club in San Francisco in 1926. His friend Upton Sinclair later wrote that Sterling had been killed by "the nebular hypothesis," referring to the poet's obsession with scientific theories of a universe wracked by the birth and death of stars, a Medusa-vision of the infinite which transformed spirit into stone:

Medusa of the light, whose deadly gaze
Shall turn the spirit, not the flesh, to stone!
Abiding shadow of the infinite!
Terror immortal, twin-born with the sun
From night's abyss! Why do men seek thy face?
For they that find thee shall not know they find;
For they that find thee shall be changed. Their hearts
Shall ache with loneliness to see thy face
Among the stars, more beautiful than they—
Among the stars, but colder than all stars,
A phantom and a goddess and a fire.

Yet Sterling, popularly dubbed the "King of Bohemia" in San Francisco, led a life of transgressive revelry and dandyism; his highly ornate poetry and persona attracted the interest of Jack London and Ambrose Bierce, who became members of his inner circle.

In London's autobiographical novel *Martin Eden*, a character modeled on Sterling explains his hedonism as an attempt to "squirm my little space in the cosmic dust whence I came." Bacchanalia were conducted by Sterling most famously in Piedmont (a suburb of Oakland), San Francisco (at Coppa's restaurant as well as the Bohemian Club), and Carmel.

The profane fervor of Sterling's bohemianism stands in direct relation to the sublime intensity of his cosmic pessimism; through Sterling's influence, a desperate Revel and a dark Revelation became mutually conditioning aspects of the Bay Area's first avant-garde.

Across the gap of the interwar years, only the merest tendrils of this decadent design extended into the fretwork of the San Francisco Renaissance and Beat scene (remaining most evident in the Romanticism of Duncan and Lamantia); with the ascendency of the anti-Romantic Language movement, the vine of Sterling's West-Coast aestheticism crumbled at last.

Even during Sterling's lifetime, however, his work never achieved a central position within American literature. Situated at the "continent's end," at the outer limits, so to speak, of national destiny, Sterling cultivated a variety of decadence that differed in taste and sensibility from those liqueurs of decay so exquisitely refined in the metropoles of the East Coast and Europe. Sterling's texts, despite their deliberately archaic diction, roil and boil with an intemperate rawness that seems to draw upon the inhuman otherness of an all-surrounding wilderness.

Nature, untamed, stalks through the works of Sterling as a "lethal void," a force beyond reckoning, whereas in the contemporaneous works of the New York decadents, nature, when considered at all, receives an Emersonian reading as a symbol for the spirit, sometimes deciphered according to a doctrine of correspondences; or else, following Oscar Wilde, "unfinished" nature is dismissed easily and ironically as an inferior imitation of Art.

But for Sterling and his circle, nature's arbitrary power over culture was demonstrated horrifically by the earthquake of 1906. No one from the circle of bohemians was killed or injured, but many of their favorite haunts, including Coppa's restaurant, were destroyed. And most of the entire second edition of Sterling's first book of poems, *Testimony of the Suns*, was lost when the publisher's warehouse burned in the citywide fire.

However, Sterling's party already had moved south, to the seaside resort of Carmel, where (as the novelist Mary Austin reported) "Sterling's greatest pleasures were those that whetted his incessant appetite for sensation—the sting of the surf against his body, the dangerous pull of the undertow off the Carmel beaches . . . " There, Sterling erected a "pagan altar" by nailing cow skulls to the trees encircling their campsite. Sterling was residing in this rustic enclave when his most celebrated poem, "A Wine of Wizardry," was published in *The Cosmopolitan* magazine in 1907.

"A Wine of Wizardry" presents a phantasmagoria of paganist, medievalist, and Orientalist scenes, a cavalcade of images cohering loosely, if at all, under the conceit of a wine-inspired flight of Fancy. Despite the imagistic extremism of the poem, Ambrose Bierce arranged for his employer Hearst's *Cosmopolitan* to publish it; in his commentary (which accompanied the poem's appearance in the magazine), Bierce defended the work's lack of emotionality and "human interest," admitting frankly that, "The verses serve no cause, tell no story, point no moral. Their author has no purpose, end, or care other than the writing of poetry."

The publication of this "pure" poem was met with incomprehension and condemnation. A long poem consisting of nothing but violent and lurid images, so unabashed in its negation of the principles of harmony and proportion, was unprecedented, as one critic asserted, "in the whole range of American, or, for that matter, English poetry." Bierce responded by arguing that Sterling had reinvented the long poem in English: instead of writing "brief poetical passages connected by long passages of metrical prose" or *recitativo*, Sterling had, with a sovereign gesture, erased the *recitativo*. "His passages of poetry are connected by passages of poetry."

The poem's formal bizarreness is matched only by the excess of its content, which amounts to a fantastic potlatch, a swirling heterology of strangeness and evil. Indeed, Sterling's poem, serving no cause, telling no story, and pointing no moral may stand as the first example in Anglo-American literature of a *sovereign* work, as Bataille defined it (in *L'Experience intérieure*) inasmuch as the text produces "excesses of energy" that "cannot be utilized. The excessive energy can only be lost without the slightest aim. . . . This useless, senseless loss *is* sovereignty."

With the publication of "A Wine of Wizardry," Sterling acquired a national reputation as an American Decadent poet. Although his relations with Bierce and London grew strained (and ended with Bierce's disappearance into Mexico in 1913 and London's death in 1916), Sterling acquired many new friends and followers as a result of his fame. An eighteen-year-old aspiring poet from Auburn, California, by the name of Clark Ashton Smith, after encountering "A Wine of Wizardry" and being overwhelmed by its "necromantic music," sent samples of his own (obviously imitative) work to Sterling.

Smith was invited to visit Sterling's circle of bohemians in Carmel, but the shy and sickly youth felt uncomfortable among the carousing company. Smith soon returned to Auburn but began to correspond with the older poet. Finally, under Sterling's mentorship, Smith amassed a book-length collection of verse; entitled *The Star-Treader and Other Poems*, the book appeared in 1912 under the imprint of Sterling's own publisher.

The critics reviewed this work in much the same manner as "A Wine of Wizardry": the "lions of reaction" (in Bierce's phrase) denounced the book for its "ghoulish" luxuriance, while others praised Smith inordinately, deeming him "the Boy Genius of the Sierras." With a line of influence clearly established, the writings of Sterling and Smith developed a distinct tradition of California Decadence, one whose invocation of cosmic otherness diverged from the more subjective varieties of aestheticism practiced in the cities of the East.

Sterling returned to San Francisco in 1918 and continued to pursue his scandal-provoking activities at the Bohemian Club, even as Smith became more reclusive and neurasthenic. Sterling reportedly offered to help place the young poet in a sanitarium, but Smith refused. In 1922, Smith decided to self-publish his new volume of verse, entitled *Ebony and Crystal*. This collection, for which Sterling wrote an introduction, includes Smith's most celebrated poem, "The Hashish-Eater; or, The Apocalypse of Evil." Described by H. P. Lovecraft as "the greatest imaginative orgy in English literature," the text constitutes both an homage to and an exponential expansion of Sterling's "A Wine of Wizardry."

. . . Silence loads
The wind of ether, and the worlds are still
To hear the word that flees me. All my dreams
Fall like a rack of fuming vapors raised
To semblance by a necromant, and leave
Spirit and sense unthinkably alone,
Above a universe of shrouded stars,
And suns that wander, cowled with sullen gloom,
Like witches to a Sabbath.

Both Sterling's wine-inspired and Smith's hashish-inspired poems are sovereign works, apocalypses of evil in which human life is rendered, as in ritual sacrifice, to the ravening flux of cosmic forces. As such, both works are driven by what Bataille has termed *imperative heterogeneity*: the poems' imagery comes in consequence of an uncontrollable dissemination. The excess of expenditure evident in the image-flow of these works multiplies and ultimately defeats meaning. Here, it is helpful to remember that the poems' vehicles of wine and hashish already have been specified by Baudelaire in *Les Par-*

adis artificiels as "means of multiplying the self" (*moyens de multiplication de l'individualité*).

Perversely, the wasteful extravagance of nature itself is imported by Sterling and Smith into cultural modalities long ago emptied and exhausted of meaning. Artificially revived, relic prosodies then walk through the worlds of "Wine" and "Hashish" as a species of living dead.

I see a tiny star within the depths—
A light that stays me, while the wings of doom
Convene their thickening thousands: For the star
Increases, taking to its hueless orb,
With all the speed of horror-changéd dreams
The light as of a million million moons;
And floating up through gulfs and glooms eclipsed,
It grows and grows, a huge white eyeless Face,
That fills the void and fills the universe,
And bloats against the limits of the world
With lips of flame that open.

The poems thus read as stream-of-consciousness without a unifying subjectivity, and present an unnatural, archaically mediated mimesis of the body's wilderness, oscillating between pleasure and pain. Is it surprising that here, at the limits of Western civilization, Sterling and Smith devised a poetics of embodiment as exquisite torture (reversing earlier Romantic representations of bliss as ascension toward a kind of Neoplatonic disembodiment)? No more surprising than that the hundred-year-old *oblivion-seeking lushness* of California Decadent poetry should outline, as a radiant silhouette, the missing body of a "post-avant" poetics.

On Neo-Surrealism

Surrealism is the practice of conjuring Otherness, of realizing the infinite negativity of desire in order to address, and to redress, the poverty of the positive fact. In Marxian terms, it demands a sensorium, a social body, capable of making the leap from the realm of necessity to the realm of freedom.

The surrealist identification of reality and desire has obvious sources in Romanticism and even earlier, alchemical and Hermetic, doctrines. However, in surrealism this identification leads, not to reconciliation, but to *agonistic embrace*— that is, to the beautiful convulsion of irresolvable paradox. For surrealism, the vertiginous spiral by which the familiar is estranged can never end in refamiliarization. The surrealist struggle has to be waged not only against society but also, scandalously, against nature. Its cosmo-political teaching heralds the establishment of a Church of Disquiet.

Still, surrealism does not levitate above History; the shape of surrealist subversion shifts according to the contours of the surrounding landscape. Both the darkness of the "uncanny" and the brightness of the "marvelous" are not absolute but relative qualities. Only at midnight does the apparition of the Sun become strange.

As Philip Lamantia, the most prominent North American surrealist, has asked: "What is not strange?" The question raises the curtain on the situation of surrealism in the New World, where everything—and so nothing—is strange. Here, in the society of the spectacle, the empowering twist of estrangement tends to reverse direction and spiral toward the passive doom of alienation. Here, the techniques of surrealism seem to have been all too readily absorbed by the advertising system.

Yet in the Old World also, surrealism was implicated in—even as it developed a radical response to—the increasing commodification of the life-world. Surrealism has enacted, since its inception, a critique and a carnival of the object under capitalism. And in doing so, it has anticipated and transcended the self-ironizing discourse of postmodern consumerism: for the object is not simply a sign to be endlessly circulated, but also a *non-sign*, the materialization of a mystery whose *non-sense* signals the irruption of the genuinely new.

In the dominant culture of the United States, otherness has been systematically denied a presence, so that the *surreal* must be perceived only as a representation of the *unreal*. Perhaps this is why those postwar American artists who fell under the influence of surrealism—Gorky, Motherwell, Pollock—tended, in their later practice, to redefine the problem of representation itself, and to reclaim the will-to-otherness as a form of the non-representational.

(No similar stratagem was undertaken by the surrealist-inspired poets of that time: Parker Tyler's verse, for example, never ventured far from Romantic metaphor. In some sense, however, an impulse toward abstraction was already evident in the most "advanced" surrealist poetry, where the imagery—the juxtaposition, according to Breton's famous citation of Reverdy, of "the most distant realities"—remains properly *non-visualizable*.)

But surrealism is not exempt from its own imperative, synthesized from Marx and Rimbaud, to "transform the world" and to "change life." Even in its earliest years, while unified under the leadership of Breton, the movement underwent successive mutations in response to internal and external conditions. The self-identity of the movement therefore cannot be situated within timeless tenets, but only in *the shock-pattern of the wave-front of surrealization as it passes, under the impetus of practices not to be prescribed in advance, through a particular time and place*. This expanding wave-front has no permanently fixed form or content. Surreality is not a state of standing "over" reality; rather, it is the boiling-over of that reality, a phase-change that always departs from a highly specific set of initial conditions. "Neo-surrealism" is a term that refuses termination—one that awaits the emergence of the *novum* within surrealism itself.[1]

1. Lamantia himself once articulated a neo-surrealist position in his statement "Between the Gulfs" (1973): "From this vista of dormant volcanos and tropical ice, we can all the more happily trace our inspirations from Lautréamont and Rimbaud to Breton and Péret and Roussel to [the Haitian poet] Magloire-Saint-Aude, exemplary signposts for further transgressions, *without literally re-tracing in one's own poetic praxis their inimitable movements* [emphasis added]."

The Revolution by Night

Control panel oil painting abandoned tenement toy piano votive candles dirty curtains—

The seven sisters. Milk anemone road map rusty pipe secret meeting—

Glare interval bottle. Spilled script. The exits leading to identical places. Advancing animal figures half formed, once invested with humanity—

"Of fled immensities, the huntress." Wheels of prophecy in public square. The hidden flaw—

That the exact vertex between noon & midnight is their flag, twin of green dusk. The simples displaced, as numbers curved past all beginning—kissed, then burnt to the follicle—

Logical afterimage: the State. Accelerated weather.

To live underwater, our clothes billowing, our hair shifting in the cold currents like seaweed—

Forgetting the social (whose booming echoes rolled over us long before birth), we are guided through soft interiors of the word *mass*, first in its medical, then religious, then astronomical uses—

This yellow bone has fallen from the Moon. All the newspapers are stamped with a new insignia of crossed pikes.

Whereas History must be steered by the four elements, the fifth is crystalline, and aligned with Tragedy—

In scales of rising similar to music—the people could not be distinguished from deserted buildings.

The Cry at Zero

The *via negativa*—a way of unknowing that leads to an encounter with that being beyond being or, better, that poses the paradox of *being beyond itself*—necessarily trespasses the limits of language. Its procedure is comparable to the poetic practice that attempts to say the unsayable.

A negative theology, by denying all sensible and intelligible attributes to divinity, brings about the de-anthropomorphization of God. So poetry, in answering its highest calling, results in the de-anthropomorphization of language.

For there are words of abandon to be uttered before the abandonment of words.

The struggle to embrace the divine, whether by words or actions, ultimately dissolves all distinction between subject and object. In this endeavor, language—the earthly integument of the soul—must arrive at an impossible space in which meaning stands outside itself, allowing the Word to come to *ekstasis*. This is the condition of absolute poetry.

Philip Lamantia, the American surrealist and author of a book of poems entitled *Ekstasis*, once was asked in an interview: "Can the poem say the unsayable?" Lamantia answered, "Isn't this what poets have always aspired to? Seemingly failing in the attempt but finally achieving *a miracle in words*."

Lamantia, while never renouncing surrealism, returned to the Catholic faith shortly before his death in 2005. This need not be surprising, given the deep, yet agonized relation of the surrealist movement itself to the Catholic milieu from which it emerged. Surrealism's road to the Absolute departs from, even as it radicalizes, the traditional Catholic emphasis on sacred embodiment.

Among the poems left unpublished by Lamantia at the time of his death, there is a sequence entitled *Tau*, dating from an earlier phase of the poet's lifelong struggle with religious devotion. The poem appears to be unfinished: the typescript is scarred with numerous and conflicting revisions. One recurrent line, "his love loveless in a cloud," recalls the famous fourteenth-century mystical text *The Cloud of Unknowing*, in which love is defined as the only bond capable of uniting human and divine being. Lamantia's refrain exemplifies the self-negating turn that meaning must take in the ascent toward *ekstasis*: within the Cloud of Unknowing, all words are to be placed under erasure, even the key word "love."

Furthermore, any word that "makes sense" in reference to finite being suffers an ontological rupture when applied to that Being beyond being. One over infinity equals zero: so too the word, in attempting to stand over—to understand—God-head, cancels itself: at the height of the cloud, "love" turns "loveless."

What is involved here is not a simple reversal of polarity, but a higher-order negation of both positive and negative meaning. Not "love," but a language-event (a meta-negation: "love loveless") breaks the membrane between human and divine being. The early Christian mystic Pseudo-Dionysius argued that such a breakthrough could occur only by "unnaming" the Divine Names: not only affirmations but denials—such as the attempt to describe God as "indescribable"—must be denied. Yet this form of "unknowing," as an act of *ekstasis*, or "standing outside," is no longer privative but projective: a knowing beyond knowing.

In Lamantia's poem, both "+love" and "-love" coincide as charged elements within the Cloud. The mystical figure of a coincidence of opposites can be represented as the point at which twinned (entwined) infinities—the self-mirroring series of positive and negative numbers—meet at zero.

This zero-point is also a crossing point, a crossing out and a crossing-over of the Sign.

As language ascends toward the divine, words acquire new and unprecedented properties that bring them into *poetic* relation with one another. Here, the unsayable nature of the divine is manifested in the speech-act itself. The mystical union does not silence, but instead *unseals* the Word.

The encounter with the Absolute must also relativize the difference between speech and silence. Likewise, to enter the space of the Absolute means ecstatically to lose one's bearings: there is finally no difference between ascent and descent. This crossing-point is a site of utter suspension, of an utterance suspended at the crux of beyond-being: the Cry at zero.

(The title of Lamantia's "lost" poem, *Tau*, reflects a poetic synthesis of zero and the sign of the cross. The Greek letter *tau* is equivalent to the Roman letter T, and has been used to signify the Christian cross. Moreover, the Greek word for "zero," tsifra, begins with this letter; consequently, *tau* also is used as an abbreviation for zero.)

This Cry out of the zeroic abyss is an articulation, not a cancellation, of silence.

It says that if something exists, it exists as the cliff and the glyph of Nothing.

Such a cry or crisis within Nothing was contemplated by certain of the German mystics, notably Jacob Boehme. Nothing, as a state of absolute freedom, is free to nullify its own identity, to cease and to seize itself, to set Nothing against Nothing and so grind against itself, to issue its own groundless (and perhaps soundless) groan. Boehme referred to this convulsive self-complication of Nothing as the *Ungrund*. He wrote: "The *Ungrund* is an eternal *Nothing*, yet it makes an eternal opening, as a *passion*; for the Nothing is a passion for something, and yet it still remains the Nothing that gives forth something; even while the passion is itself the giving-forth of Nothing, although what it gives is nothing other than a sheerly wanting passion" (*Mysterium pansophicum* [1620], my translation).[1]

The Absolute, as the purely unconditioned, is that which finds itself wanting any condition. Hence the structural failure of Nothing, hence its self-torment and ecstatic fall. Poetry, then, may be defined as the representation in language of this absolute Emergency.

Boehme himself represented the passion of Nothing as a musical chord of morphemes in German: *Quelle, Qual, Qualität.* That is, the ineffable Source (*Quelle*) reflects itself, and so divides in pain (*Qual*). This ontic pain underlies, indeed sustains, all conditionality (as the *Qual* in *Qualität*). While the etymology is false, the sonic signature that Boehme discovered here, the trace of the groundless Mystery in language, is true—in the way that poetry is true.

Yet the Cry at zero, representing the emergency of Nothing as a sonic (and ultimately poetic) sign, can be conceived scientifically as well. In the twentieth century, the cosmologist Edward P. Tryon speculated that the universe may have arisen as a sort of "vacuum fluctuation" (see "Is the Universe a Vacuum Fluctuation?" in *Nature*, vol. 246 [1973], pp. 396–97). At the moment of this convulsion of the vacuum, all physical values would have soared to infinity (the "infinitely hot, infinitely dense" state known as the Big Bang).

The vacuum fluctuation, a destabilization of the zero-energy

1. "Der *Ungrund* ist ein ewig *Nichts*, und machet aber einen ewigen Anfang, als eine *Sucht*; denn das Nichts ist eine Sucht nach Etwas: und da doch auch Nichts ist, das Etwas gebe; sondern die Sucht ist selber das Geben dessen, das doch auch nichts ist als bloss eine begehrende Sucht."

field, resulted not in a flash of light, but in an inhuman Cry of sound. For even as infinity poured forth from zero, light could not propagate as readily as sound within the extreme density of the primordial medium. According to a team of cosmologists writing in *Scientific American* (February 2004), it was "the pattern of density variations caused by the sound waves" that gave rise to large-scale structures, zones of compression and rarefaction that eventually coalesced into stars and galaxies. (By that time, the primordial medium had attenuated sufficiently for the universe to become transparent to light: nonetheless, *sound* had already imprinted its pattern on the background radiation.)

This Cry, in its groundlessness, is heard as a (n)ever-arriving wave, the ecstatic signal of being-beyond-itself, as it passes from the noumenon (the Nothing) to the phenomenon.

It is heard in human speech as O, the grieving vowel; and in mathematics and the speech of inhuman things as o, the sign of zero. Any value divided by zero equals infinity, so the Cry must be written as O / o.

How can Nothing be present to itself as something? Only as *the slash of division*.

The Cry enters the realm of conditional being, but only as a cry against condition as such. Thus, it is *sovereign* in the sense that Georges Bataille intended: "sovereignty is rebellion. It is not the exercise of power. Authentic sovereignty refuses" (see the concluding essay in his *Somme athéologique*, vol. 1 [1954]).

Where power imposes the law of identity, a "sheerly wanting passion" reveals its wound. The revelation of O / o is always anti-systematic, inasmuch as it represents the Opening to Otherness within a given order. As sigh or sign resisting the empire of being, the Cry is heard soundlessly as intervallic suspension; or, as irruptive alterity, it rings out like a gong that shatters with its own vibration.

Emergency everlasting.

ALSO BY ANDREW JORON

Poetry
Science Fiction (Berkeley: Pantograph Press, 1992)
The Removes (West Stockbridge, Massachusetts: Hard Press, 1999)
Fathom (New York: Black Square Editions, 2003)

Criticism
*The Sun at Night: Transformations of Surrealism in American Poetry,
    1966–1999* (New York: Black Square Editions, 2004)

Translation
Ernst Bloch, *Literary Essays* (Stanford, California: Stanford Univer-
    sity Press, 1998)
Richard Anders, *The Footsteps of One Who Has Not Stepped Forth*
    (New York: Black Square Editions, 2000)

Andrew Joron was born in San Antonio, Texas, in 1955 and grew up in Stuttgart, Germany; Lowell, Massachusetts; and Missoula, Montana. He attended the University of California at Berkeley, where he majored in history and philosophy of science. After a decade and a half spent writing science-fiction poetry, culminating in his volume *Science Fiction* (1992), he turned to a more philosophical mode of speculative lyric. This work has been collected in *The Removes* (1999) and in *Fathom* (2003). He is also the translator, from the German, of the Marxist-Utopian philosopher Ernst Bloch's *Literary Essays* (1998), and of the surrealist Richard Anders's aphorisms and prose poems. Andrew Joron lives in Berkeley, where he works as a freelance bibliographer and indexer.